The
Dressage Competitors'
Handbook

The Dressage Competitors' Handbook

Suzanne K. B. Fraser

Foreword by Cindy Sydnor

Equissentials Press

The Dressage Competitors' Handbook

Library of Congress Catalog Card Number: 99-97568

Fraser, Suzanne K. B.
    The Dressage Competitors' Handbook

ISBN 0-9654900-1-7

Disclaimer of Liability

❧ *Dedication* ❧

To my husband

Douglas A. Fraser

Although it's customary to only list the name of the person to whom a book is dedicated, it would be inadequate to do so under the circumstances. Doug has been a driving force and supporter of this project from start to finish and put aside his own projects in order to help me complete this book. He took many of the pictures that appear here, created all of the arena diagrams, kept my computer and printer running when they threatened to take unscheduled vacations, and acted as a reliable sounding board on hundreds of occasions. This book is far better thanks to his unselfish and significant contributions.

Acknowledgements

I'm not sure that there is any way to adequately acknowledge and thank everyone who has contributed directly or indirectly to this book. It was a big undertaking and would not have been possible without the generosity and kindness of everyone listed below. I can just hope that they all derive some satisfaction from seeing the project completed. My sincerest thanks to all of you!

Special thanks go to:

My parents, Linton P. Bell and Sally C. Bell, for their unflagging support, encouragement, and generosity.

Sara B. Fraser, my stepdaughter and editor extraordinaire.

Susan S. Sellew, my very dear friend, for her editorial contributions and moral support over many, many years.

Cindy Sydnor. Originally, I asked Cindy if she would be willing to write a foreword for me. Ultimately, she went well beyond that by providing me with some very nice photographs and valuable editorial comments.

Thanks are also due the following people (in alphabetical order):

Samuel Barish, president of the USDF, from stepping in at a critical moment to assist me.

Dan Brown, USDF'S Director of Administration, for his assistance with information pertaining to the USDF'S awards programs.

Patti Carey-Stedman for her significant contribution to the chapter, *Care and Feeding of the Dressage Competitor: Your Horse and You.* And for helping me keep my sense of humor and my perspective when various issues threatened to disturb both.

Patricia L. Goodman for her beautiful photographs and vote of confidence.

Merri-Lyn L. Griffin for her technical expertise with *Appendix A.*

Helenikos for being so patient and good-natured as we "dressed him up" and made him pose for photos.

Kyra Beth Houston and Dressage Unlimited (www.dressageunltd.com) for assistance with the numerous acronyms associated with dressage organizations and for information provided regarding selection trials.

Cecelia Hoyt (owner of Windfal). My thanks to Cecelia for the use of "Windy's" picture and of her beautiful farm where many of the pictures of Susan Russell were taken.

Kathryn King Johnson for her assistance with the chapter, *Warming Up and Warm-Up Area Etiquette.*

Sophie Leimer and the FEI for their assistance with the many acronyms associated with international dressage competition.

Kathy Mann, owner of Mannuscript Farm, home of the Oldenburg stallion *Mannhattan*, for her moral support, good advice, and sympathetic ear.

Candace T. Piscopo, owner/rider of Nebraska.

Ruth Hogan Poulsen, rider of Aristocrat.

Elizabeth Ritz, owner of Aristocrat.

Susan Russell, owner/rider of Daktara and rider of Windfal.

Eliza Sydnor, rider of Double K.

Preface

Not long ago I was at a dressage schooling show with a friend who was venturing into the world of competition for the first time. She had been working diligently at home to ensure that she was ready for the introductory level tests, she knew the correct method for saluting, knew how to turn herself and her horse out appropriately, and was mentally prepared — or as much as any person new to the competition scene can be.

I had talked to her about warming up around the outside of the arena and giving her horse the opportunity to see the judge's booth from both directions, but I had neglected to mention the one-minute rule. So, when the judge rang the bell, she looked at me with a startled expression and asked, "What do I do now?"

That single question made me think of the numerous rules (written and unwritten) surrounding dressage competitions, and it occurred to me that there was no single source containing this information. I decided to see if I could make dressage showing a little easier and more understandable to dressage competitors and spectators by compiling this information in one place.

With that said, I hope this book serves to answer all of your basic questions and maybe a few that you didn't even know you had. Showing is supposed to be fun and educational — and it is much more enjoyable if you feel adequately prepared.

Much of the fun in showing is that you learn something new and valuable at every show, sometimes from your own rides and sometimes by watching others ride. I urge you to spectate whenever possible so that you don't miss out on good learning experiences, and I look forward to seeing you at the next dressage show.

Contents

Foreword

There have been so many seemingly simple great ideas that we say to ourselves, "Why didn't I think of that?" Suzy Fraser has come up with one of those ideas. Here is a compilation of everything you need to know about competing in dressage. Like many readers, I laughed as I read, thinking how much simpler my life as a competitor would have been, especially in the beginning, if I had had a book such as this.

Everything you need to know about competing — from preparation at home, lists of what to take for your horse and yourself, how and when to fill out and mail your entry form, correct attire, how to salute, how to warm up, how to relax, and much more — is here. Read this book before you go to a show, and keep a copy in your truck, for it is full of important and interesting information. It is one of the best gifts you could give to a new competitor — or to an experienced competitor. I plan to keep it nearby for my students and myself.

The book is well organized, logical, and easy to read. If you have a question about any aspect of showing in dressage, you will find the answer here. The advice is often technical, such as "How long can the whip be?" And there are practical solutions to technical problems, such as "How can I shorten my whip?" But there is more here, too, including excellent advice on how to determine the level and tests you should select, warm-up area etiquette, and information on the various award programs.

I am sure that show secretaries and managers will be glad this book exists, as I am, and as I'm sure you will be. Many thanks to Suzy for putting all this information together.

Best wishes, Cindy Sydnor

Enter at A

Everyone planning to compete wants to be well prepared so that they can put in their best possible effort and avoid making mistakes. Good preparation goes well beyond your horse's and your training although those are essential ingredients. In addition, you should understand:

- The different levels.
- What level you should enter.
- The show's rules and regulations.
- How to prepare for a show.
- The proper tack and attire.
- Warm up area etiquette.
- How to complete the entry form.
- The basics of test riding.
- How to care for your horse and yourself in a competition setting.
- How scoring works.
- How to care for your horse after the show.

You must know how to salute, be aware of the one-minute rule, know how to turn onto the centerline, and much more. This book covers these

Whenever you encounter an unfamiliar term, refer to the Glossary at the end of the book.

important areas in an easy-to-understand format so that you will feel well prepared as you tackle your first dressage shows. It can also serve as a quick reference as needed.

Although all of the levels are explained in the chapter entitled *Understanding the Levels*, the primary focus of this book is on the lower levels since these are the levels in which the majority of newcomers compete.

It is your responsibility as a competitor to learn the rules and regulations for dressage competitions. Failure to do so could lead to problems including elimination.

This book provides all the information you need to start your competition career as well as recommendations on other available resources for expanding your knowledge. You will be able to compete confidently knowing that you have the information you need in order to enjoy a successful and educational experience.

Competing - Why We Do It

When deciding whether to compete, it is important to consider your own personal goals and reasons for competing. There are many reasons to compete. Your reasons may include some or all of the following:

- To get an objective opinion of your training from a qualified judge.
- To see how your horse and you compare to other horses and riders at your level.
- To evaluate your progress over a period of time with the help of the judges.
- To pursue year end awards through USDF, AHSA, and regional and breed organizations.
- To promote yourself (as a trainer, instructor, judge, clinician, etc.).
- To promote your farm (boarding, training, and selling).
- To promote a horse you are selling.
- To promote a stallion you are standing.
- To spend time with other people who share your love of horses.
- To watch the upper level horses and riders.
- For the fun of it!

Any type of athletic competition requires dedication, hard work, and a lot of practice. However, competing in dressage requires more preparation than most sports because there are two of you: you are not only working to perfect your own skills, but you are simultaneously working on improving your horse.

Although a competition may seem like one isolated moment in time, it is actually a cumulation of the months and years that have gone into the training of every horse and rider. Obviously, the riders who dutifully apply themselves to the study of riding — both in theory and in practice — will enjoy greater competitive success than those who pursue riding casually.

Competing requires an enormous amount of effort, and at the end of the day, the most you may have to show for it is a ribbon and maybe some photographs. Nonetheless, a lot of people are anxious to get out there and give it a try. Competing is exhausting, frustrating, expensive, and tests our limits as riders and trainers. But it's also educational, inspirational, and a lot of fun. To make it worthwhile and as much fun as possible, you should be well prepared. Knowledge and proper preparation are the key to success — not only knowledge of riding and training, but of handling everything that the experience of competition presents.

Competitive Success is Based on Habituation

If you have been attentive and committed along the way, then competitive success won't have anything to do with luck; instead it will be a testimonial to the time you have devoted to correct training and careful preparation. This constant attention to detail is a process known as habituation. Every time you ride, you should ride to the best of your ability. If you strive to develop good riding habits and solid basics, then you will be well prepared when it comes time to compete. You will have a firm foundation that gives you the best chance of succeeding.

If something should go amiss in competition, chances are it will be due to inexperience on your horse's or your part, or to a missing piece in your training. Either way, view it as a learning experience and a challenge — something you can work on to improve.

By holding yourself to a certain level of excellence in your daily riding, you are doing what is best for your horse and yourself. And when you do go

Constant attention to detail is a process known as habituation.

out to compete, the only difference will be that you are riding in a different location. You will be relaxed because you are confident in your horse's and your abilities.

If you are interested in competition as a way to evaluate how you are doing, rather than just winning, then all the steps along the way will offer their own rewards and enjoyment. Since you will devote hundreds of hours of work relative to the number of minutes you actually compete, it's important that you enjoy the daily process.

Don't forget that your horse needs fun and variety just as much as you. Trotting poles, caveletti, jumping, hacking, and other activities are all useful for developing your dressage horse physically while keeping him happy and interested in his work. Lisa Goodman on a cross-country course with the Trakehner stallion Peron. Photo: Patricia L. Goodman

Dressage Is for Every Breed, Every Rider

Dressage is a French word that means *training*. Every horse — whether intended for dressage, jumping, reining, trail riding, or any other discipline — needs training. Advocates of different styles of riding promote different training methods, but generally we all subscribe to some basic tenets: we want horses that are trusting, willing, obedient, and happy partners. To this end, we labor many hours to learn how best to achieve these goals.

Dressage can be the end in itself or it can be the means to an end. Some riders are dedicated to the sport and will pursue it to the highest level of their horse's and their ability. Other riders use dressage as a way to improve the suppleness, obedience, and adjustability of their horses for another discipline entirely. Jumper riders are a good example. They must be able to easily extend their horse's canter in order to make the best possible time around a course, but they must also be able to collect the horse for a tight corner or to negotiate a particular type of fence. This adjustability must be

Cecelia Hoyt's purebred Arabian gelding, Windfal, started his career as a driving horse. Susan Russell (shown In photo) trained and competed him in dressage to the FEI levels. "Windy" now enjoys semi-retirement at Cecelia's farm in Vermont.

done quickly and gracefully to maximize performance. Dressage is a great way to improve these qualities.

Although certain breeds and conformation types may find dressage work easier than others, every horse can benefit from the systematic and progressive nature of dressage. A trail rider will especially appreciate a horse that easily performs a turn on the forehand and then stands quietly while she opens or closes a gate. A polo player must have a horse that will ignore a mallet being swung around his body and concentrate on his rider's aids for turns and transitions, which happen quickly and frequently.

Dressage is beneficial to horses with less than ideal conformation. A horse that is built downhill (the horse's croup is higher than his withers) will benefit by learning to shift more of his weight onto his hind legs. Not only does this make for a more comfortable ride, but it also helps in preserving the horse's soundness. The horse that is long in the back and doesn't track up will benefit by learning better engagement. These are just a few examples of the many benefits of dressage.

Dressage serves to improve the suppleness, obedience, balance, strength, and adjustability of the horse so that he is a pleasure to ride and retains his soundness over many years. For the rider, dressage teaches us to be in balance and harmony with our horses, understanding of their basic instincts and needs, and empathic to them as our friends and partners.

Who Can Compete in Dressage?

Riders of all ages, male or female, can enjoy and compete in dressage. It provides a good, solid basis for any rider who wants to develop a better seat no matter what discipline they ultimately choose to pursue, and it's appealing to anyone who enjoys precision and grace.

Horses of any breed, type, or sex can compete in dressage. However, there are important competition age requirements as follows:

- A horse must be at least 36 months of age to compete.
- Horses competing above Fourth level must be at least 6 years of age.
- Horses competing at Grand Prix must be at least 7 years of age.

Ponies are prohibited from competing in USET Championships and USET qualifying and selection trials, and observation classes.

A horse's age is counted from January 1 of the year of birth to January 1 of the current competition year.

Understanding the Levels

The most basic level of dressage competition is Introductory level. The Introductory level tests are written by the United States Dressage Federation (USDF) and are seen primarily at schooling shows. Occasionally, a recognized competition will offer Introductory level, but scores earned at Introductory level do not count toward any year end awards.

After Introductory level are Training, First, Second, Third, and Fourth with Training being the most basic and Fourth level the most difficult. These are U.S. levels, and all the tests for these levels are written by the American Horse Shows Association (AHSA).

The most advanced levels are the Federation Equestre Internationale (FEI) levels. In ascending order, they are — Prix St Georges, Intermediaire I, Intermediaire II, Grand Prix, and the Grand Prix Special. These tests are written by the FEI and are used worldwide.

Each of the lower levels, from Introductory through Fourth, contains several different tests. Test 1 is always the first and easiest test within a level. Each subsequent test asks for a higher degree of difficulty, new movements, or both.

Schooling shows are small, local competitions that are not usually recognized by the AHSA or USDF. They are typically organized by local clubs or farms to give novice riders, or riders with green horses, some competition experience in a relaxed setting. Although schooling shows may not be recognized by the AHSA, most adhere to AHSA rules or slightly amended AHSA rules.

Tests are designed to encourage correct training that will serve to improve a horse's gaits and obedience while developing him at a rate that will not compromise his soundness. The levels and tests within each level are intended to lead the horse and rider forward gradually and logically. Not only is each level more difficult than its predecessor, but each test within a particular level asks more difficult questions of the horse and rider.

The levels are explained below. Not all levels have the same number of tests within them as shown in parentheses next to each level. Training, First, and Second levels all contain four tests, with Test 1 being the simplest. Third and Fourth levels offer three tests each.

The Levels

One of the first things you should do since you are contemplating competing is to get copies of the tests for the level at which you are interested in showing. As you will see by reading the tests, each level builds on the one before it by asking for new movements or by increasing the difficulty of familiar movements. For instance, by changing from 20-meter circles in Training level to 15-meter circles in First level, the degree of difficulty is increased, thus requiring a higher degree of training. At First level, leg yielding and trot and canter lengthenings are also introduced.

Precision becomes increasingly important at each progressive level, as do the degrees of suppleness, straightness, collection, and extension. Where it was acceptable in Training level to perform a halt through the walk, at First level the horse is expected to perform a smooth transition from the trot to the halt and the halt to the trot, with no walk steps.

USDF Tests

Introductory Level (Tests 1 and 2)

Introductory level is the most basic level and is designed to introduce young horses or inexperienced riders to the competition environment. These tests are typically offered at schooling shows but are sometimes offered at USDF/AHSA recognized shows. All work is performed in the walk and trot, and no halt is required at the beginning of either test. USDF does not offer any awards programs for Introductory level.

You can get copies of any of the AHSA tests by contacting the AHSA directly. Their address is AHSA, Inc., 220 East 42nd Street, New York, NY 10017-5876. Tel. 212-972-2472

The Collective Marks (the marks that appear at the bottom of the score sheet) in the Introductory level tests are different than those in the AHSA or FEI tests. The coefficients for the collective marks at Introductory level appear in the far right column of the table below.

Gaits	*Freedom and regularity*	*1*
Impulsion	*Desire to move forward, relaxation of the back*	*2*
Submission	*Attention and confidence; harmony, lightness and ease of movements; acceptance of the bit*	*3*
Rider's position and seat	*Correctness and effect of the aids*	*3*

See the chapter entitled *Scoring* for detailed information on coefficients.

AHSA Tests

Training Level (Tests 1 through 4)

These tests include walk, trot, and canter work, and all circles are 20-meters in diameter. In Tests 1 and 2, the trot work can be performed at the sitting trot, rising trot, or a combination of the two. Tests 3 and 4 include movements that specifically call for the sitting trot. The mandatory sitting trot in tests 3 and 4 serve to increase the level of difficulty of these tests.

In all four Training level tests, transitions to the halt may be made through the walk. At this level, the judge wants to see that the horse is supple, relaxed, and accepting contact with the bit. Circles should be round and accurate, and transitions should be smooth.

First Level (Tests 1 through 4)

First level builds on the foundation laid in Training level and asks for some new and more difficult movements. Trot and canter lengthenings are introduced to demonstrate that the horse has developed some pushing power, while trot leg yields demonstrate the horse's suppleness and willingness to move away from the rider's leg. A trot serpentine is included in Test 1 to demonstrate that the horse is supple enough to easily change from one bend to another. A canter loop is included in Test 4 to introduce the horse to counter canter, and circles are now 15-meters in diameter. To perform the smaller circles, counter canter loop, trot and canter lengthenings, and leg yield, the horse must be more balanced, more supple, and have more pushing power than at Training level.

Second Level (Tests 1 through 4)

The transition from First to Second level is significant and not to be undertaken lightly. At Second level the horse must show collection in the trot and canter for the first time and is asked to perform medium trot and canter. In addition, a number of new movements are introduced including turn on the haunches, shoulder-in, travers, and reinback. The horse must perform counter canter, walk to canter transitions, and 10-meter circles at the trot and canter.

> Collected and medium gaits first appear at Second level. As one moves up the levels, a higher degree of collection in the collected gaits and more expression in the medium and extended gaits are expected.

At this point, the horse is expected to demonstrate more bend, balance, and carrying power than ever before.

Third Level (Tests 1 through 3)

At Third level, a higher degree of collection is required than at second level, and extended trot and canter are introduced. Added to the horse's repertoire are trot and canter half passes, 8-meter circles, walk pirouettes, and single flying changes. The rider must always remember that the quality of the gaits is foremost in importance.

Fourth Level (Tests 1 through 3)

At Fourth level, three tempi changes are asked for at every third and fourth stride, and quarter and half pirouettes in canter are introduced. Fourth level is considered medium difficulty and segues to Prix St Georges, which is the first of the FEI levels. Starting with Fourth level, all tests begin with collected canter down the centerline.

The Collective Marks for the AHSA levels (Training through Fourth)as well as the FEI levels are shown in the table at the end of this chapter with their coefficients in the far right column.

Other AHSA Tests

Other AHSA tests include:

- Quadrille
- Pas de Deux
- Musical Freestyles
- FEI Juniors — Team and Individual Tests
- FEI Young Riders — Team and Individual Tests

FEI Tests

The FEI tests are Prix St Georges, Intermediaire I (I-1), Intermediaire II (I-11), Grand Prix, and Grand Prix Special.

Prix St Georges

Prix St Georges follows Fourth level and increases the level of difficulty in the flying changes by requiring five changes at every fourth stride on one diagonal and five flying changes at every third stride on another diagonal. Half pirouettes in canter appear in Prix St Georges. 10-meter half circles in counter canter are also introduced.

Intermediaire I

The trot zigzag is introduced in the I-1 test. The five-loop canter serpentine with four of the loops in true canter, one loop in counter canter, and a flying change when crossing the centerline is introduced at I-1. Flying changes at every second stride are also required for the first time at I-1.

Intermediaire II

Passage and piaffe appear for the first time at I-II, as do the canter zigzag and flying changes at every stride.

Grand Prix and Grand Prix Special

The Grand Prix and Grand Prix Special are the ultimate test of both horse and rider. Everything required in Intermediaire II appears in Grand Prix, but with a higher degree of difficulty. For example, the I-II test calls for seven to eight steps of piaffe; at Grand Prix the horse must show 12 to 15 steps. While nine flying changes at every stride are required at I-II, the Grand Prix horse must show 15 flying changes at every stride.

The piaffe is the ultimate expression of collection.

The Writing and Designing of Tests

Every four years, the AHSA enlists a group of judges and dressage riders to review and revise Training through Fourth level tests as needed. A lot of time, energy, and talent go into the writing of these tests in an effort to be fair to both horse and rider and to encourage proper training. The people who work on revising the tests actually ride the tests to make sure that they are appropriate and offer the right challenges at the right time.

The FEI is responsible for rewriting Prix St Georges, Intermediaire I, Intermediaire II, Grand Prix, and the Grand Prix Special, and they are re-written every four years.

The only tests written and revised by the USDF are the Introductory level tests.

Some Dressage Factoids

- "Directives" are instructions that appear on the test sheet. They indicate to the judge and the rider the quality sought in a particular movement. For example, in AHSA 1999 Training level Test 1, movement 4 calls for a 20-meter canter circle on the left lead at A. The directive for this movement is "Quality of canter, roundness of circle." The judge will be looking for a nice, regular, three beat canter and a circle that is round and the correct size. It is very important for riders to review and understand these directives.
- "Coefficients" (see the chapter entitled *Scoring* for more detailed information) are assigned to particular movements to emphasize their importance in the horse's training. Any movement on a test that has a "2" to the right of it is a coefficient movement, meaning that the score is multiplied by 2.
- "Collective marks" are the marks that appear at the bottom of the test sheet. There are four individual collective marks that take into account Gaits, Impulsion, Submission, and Rider's Seat and Position. From Training level through Grand Prix, all of the collective marks carry a coefficient of 2.

Since tests are reviewed and revised every four years, be sure that you have the most current tests. Information contained in this book is based on the 1999 tests.

The Collective Marks: Training — Grand Prix

Gaits	*Freedom and regularity*	*2*
Impulsion	*Desire to move forward, elasticity of the steps, suppleness of the back, engagement of the hindquarters*	*2*
Submission	*Attention and confidence; harmony, lightness and ease of movements; acceptance of the bridle*	*2*
Rider's position	*Correctness and effect of the aids and seat*	*2*

The Canter Pirouette

Ruth Hogan Poulsen riding Elizabeth Ritz's Aristocrat.
Photo: Mary Phelps

The Purpose of the Movements

Test movements are not performed just for the fun of it — although they are a lot of fun — or because they look beautiful — although they do. Instead, movements serve a greater purpose; to improve the horse's three basic gaits. They also provide for a logical progression of training that encourages proper physical development of the horse from the standpoint of both increased flexibility and increased musculature. This helps to ensure the horse's long-term soundness, as well as his willingness to perform the work we ask of him. Movements are powerful training tools when used correctly and at the right time.

The great masters discovered that certain movements improve a horse's balance, suppleness, strength, collection, and adjustability. For example, leg yielding is a very good suppling exercise while shoulder-in is a good collecting and bending exercise. Transitions develop the horse's pushing and carrying power, while changes of gait or within the gait can be beneficial for "refreshing" a horse.

To progress through the levels, it's essential to instill good, solid basics in the horse's training so that he is both physically and mentally prepared for the more challenging work. As top trainers will attest, constant attention to the basics is essential to the rider who wants to progress with his horse; the movements are the icing. Further, if anything should go awry in the horse's schooling, the thinking rider will always return to the basics and gradually work his way back up to the problematic movement using appropriate exercises that address whatever difficulty was encountered.

The systematic, progressive training of the horse has a multitude of benefits including:

- Improving the horse's balance, which leads to better self carriage.
- Developing and improving the horse's gaits.
- Suppling the horse.
- Increasing the horse's muscle mass and strength.
- Improving the horses's obedience to the aids, thereby making him safer and more fun to ride.
- Improving the short and long term health and soundness of the horse.

The movements included in dressage tests are all movements that come naturally to the horse. Even an untrained youngster will demonstrate a lofty passage or an expressive extended trot when loose in the field and feeling good. Of course, to perform these movements with a rider takes enormous strength and training, which is why the extended trot, for example, does not show up until third level, and passage does not show up until Intermediaire II.

The various movements are introduced progressively to accommodate the horse's development and to avoid overtaxing him physically or mentally. Because of this, every rider should be aware of the training scale.

The Training Scale for the Horse

The great masters have passed down to us their immense knowledge acquired over hundreds of years and proven with numerous horses. They learned through extensive study that we should follow a particular path in training our horses — and they developed that path. Their methods have been proven repeatedly by riders with the patience and passion to develop their horses correctly.

There are many good books that explain the training scale in elaborate detail, so the following is a brief outline only. However, every dedicated

Ruth and Aristocrat performing a powerful extended trot. Notice that Aristocrat is reaching well under himself and that the cannon bone of his right hind leg is parallel to the forearm of his left front leg. Further, his poll is the highest point as it should be. Photo: Terri Miller

horse person should read up on the training scale to gain an in depth understanding of it. The basic elements of the training scale are:

• Rhythm
• Relaxation/Suppleness
• Contact
• Impulsion
• Straightness
• Collection

The Training Scale for the Rider

The rider's training scale is every bit as important as the horse's. The basic elements of the rider's training scale are:

Balance – the rider's ability to align his body correctly so that he is in balance with the horse and does not interfere with the horse's natural way of going. The rider learns to follow the horse's movement with his seat, hips, and hands, and to sit upright without being stiff or tense. A straight line can be drawn from the rider's ear to elbow to hip to heel, and from his elbow through his wrist to the bit.

Dynamic balance – the rider's ability to maintain balance while simultaneously being able to influence the horse through the correct application of the aids. The rider is aware that the horse's back moves up and down as well as side to side and is able to harmoniously follow the movement. The rider is able to influence the size of the horse's stride as well as the tempo through the use of his hips.

Application of the basic aids – the basic (natural) aids include the seat, legs, weight, hands, and voice. The artificial aids are the whip and spur and can be used to supplement the natural aids. Through proper coordination of the natural aids, the rider can perform basic movements with the horse such as going forward, turning, and stopping.

Application of the more advanced aids – Over time, the rider learns to fine tune his aids in order to ask the horse for higher degrees of collection and extension, lateral movements, transitions within the gaits, and the flying changes. The rider has much greater directional control over the horse through the use of his weight and hips and has reached a level of skill in which the artificial aids can be of use to him. As an example, the rider may give an aid through his seat, legs, and hands to ask the horse for a higher degree of collection and then enhance these natural aids by giving the horse a touch with the stick behind the [rider's] leg. This encourages the horse to use his abdominal muscles more and to bend the joints of his hind legs to a higher degree, thereby, creating a higher degree of collection.

The rider's ability to ride with his mind – Through their many interactions, both on the ground and in the saddle, riders learn the nature of horses and use this knowledge to their advantage. The rider becomes aware that horses have a natural tendency to anticipate. Rather than fighting this tendency, riders use this knowledge to achieve their goals. For instance, if the horse tends to become "more alert" (or even spooky) at a particular point in the ring, the thinking rider doesn't struggle to make the horse submit. Instead, he uses the horse's extra energy and heightened awareness to ask for a little more self-carriage and brilliance in whatever gait he is schooling.

Suggested Reading

Erik Herbermann, *Dressage Formula*
W. Museler, *Riding Logic*
Jane Savoie, *Cross Training Your Horse* and *More Cross Training*
Waldemar Seunig, *Horsemanship*
Walter Zettl, *Dressage in Harmony*

Caring for Tack and Clothing

It's important to look your best when competing as a sign of respect for your horse, yourself, and the judge. Clean clothes and tack will go far towards making a good impression and giving you that extra bit of self-confidence when competing.

Good tack care has more benefits than just keeping things looking nice — it increases the longevity of your equipment. You are also much more likely to notice if something is badly worn or about to break if you clean your tack regularly; you can have your equipment repaired before it turns into a safety issue. Billet straps, reins, stirrup leathers, and girths should be checked especially carefully.

Proper cleaning as well as appropriate storage is essential to the longevity of your equipment. Tack represents a significant financial investment, and for this reason, you will want to do your best to give it the care it needs.

Cleaning Leather

Although there is more than one way to clean tack, the method described here effectively cleans the tack and helps preserve it.

When cleaning bridles, remove straps from their runners and keepers. Use clean, warm water and a sponge to remove dirt. Once the dirt has been removed, apply saddle soap with a damp sponge, being careful not to get the leather soapy. If there are soapsuds on the leather, this indicates that there is too much water in your sponge, which can have a drying effect on your equipment. Rinse your sponge and change your wash water frequently so that you aren't just moving dirt around on your tack.

Tack only needs oiling very occasionally. If it looks or feels dry, you can oil it lightly. Be sure to wipe off any excess oil so that it doesn't stain your clothing. Most people tend to over oil tack, which can break down the fibers as well as cause a mess on your breeches and gloves. Regular cleaning as described above will help keep the proper amount of moisture and suppleness in the leather. Equipment should be cleaned after each use. Equipment that is used infrequently should be inspected regularly — storage areas that are too dry can dry out and crack leather while humid storage areas can lead to mildew. Neither is desirable.

Polishing Metal

Polishing bits, spurs, stirrups, and hardware on your tack greatly enhances the appearance of them and prevents, or at least retards, the corrosion process. A number of good metal polishes exist. Follow the directions that accompany whichever type of polish you choose.

There are flavored polishes available for use on the mouthpiece of bits. They are expensive and not your only option. Regular metal polish works fine as long as you rinse the bit well under hot water afterwards. Dry it thoroughly and you're done. The bit will be shiny but without any after taste that your horse might find objectionable.

Washing Saddle Pads

Rinse saddle pads thoroughly to ensure that all soap residue that might irritate the horse's skin is removed.

Saddle pads should be cleaned frequently following the manufacturer's instructions. This is not just for appearance's sake but to protect your horse's skin. A buildup of dirt and grime on the saddle pad can cause discomfort and possibly health problems for your horse. When a pad is damp from sweat, turn it upside down and place it somewhere that it can air dry. When dry, use a dandy brush to remove hair and dried sweat.

If you do not have the manufacturer's instructions on laundering, you can't go too far astray by washing the pad in cold water with a mild soap. If it's extremely soiled, wash it twice. Hang to dry to avoid shrinkage or having the pad dry to an unusual shape. For horses with particularly sensitive skin, run the pad through the rinse cycle twice to be sure that no soap residue remains.

Clothing Care

Riding clothes also represent a large investment and should be cared for accordingly. Dry clean your jacket after every show and store it in a breathable, fabric garment bag. Keep a small brush and a clean cloth handy at shows to clean your jacket as needed. It will undoubtedly get dust, horse slobber, or both on it during the course of the day. Use a dampened rag to clean off slobber and the brush to rid it of dust.

Avoid crossing your legs when wearing breeches to prevent polish from rubbing off on and staining them.

Stock ties, shirts, and breeches should also be laundered after each use to keep them looking clean and fresh. Many people are opting for riding tights for showing since they are less expensive and considerably easier to care for than the full leather seat breeches. Follow the laundering instructions provided and be sure to iron stock ties and shirts. Breeches can be ironed according to their fit and fabric: the stretchy, close-fitting breeches smooth out when worn. Cotton, looser fitting, and most pleated-front breeches will require ironing.

Full leather seat breeches and leather gloves can be cleaned in a number of ways, and you should check the manufacturer's instructions to see what they recommend. One method that works quite well is to turn the breeches inside out, rub mink oil paste on the leather area, and wash them in cold water with a combination of Woolite and Murphy's Oil Soap (liquid form) on the gentle cycle. Hang the breeches to dry and occasionally roll the legs up and down so that the leather remains soft and flexible as it dries. There are specific leather cleaning products available, but they do tend to be expensive. The above-described method is less expensive and works just as well.

Staying Clean at the Show

Between handling your horse, getting equipment in and out of your car and trailer, carrying water buckets, and all else that you must do at a show, it's a

Do not dry any leather goods (clothing or tack) near a direct source of heat as it can dry and crack the leather.

challenge to stay clean. If you have a long time between tests, you are well-advised to change into shorts, blue jeans, or whatever is most comfortable. Otherwise, protect your clothes by covering them with a long wraparound skirt, cotton surgeon's pants (available at many large department stores), or sweat pants if the weather is chilly. One of the worst culprits for ruining breeches is the trailer hitch, which should be greased; take extra care when moving about it. Grease always seems to find its way onto any white or light colored clothing.

Cleaning and Storing Hats

Hats should be kept covered when not in use. When you are finished riding, use a slightly dampened rag to lift dirt away from the hat. Later on, take a dry towel and wipe the hat gently to smooth out the fabric. Keep it in a plastic bag or a proper hatbox if you have one. If you have a top hat but no hatbox, find a sturdy cardboard box in which to store your hat.

Caring for Boots

Boots with a mirror finish will set you apart from the crowd. They make a positive impression on judges and spectators alike. If you use your everyday boots as your show boots, which many people do, you will need to take especially good care of them. If possible, avoid wearing them when you are grooming or doing barn chores. Put them on right before you mount up and take them off as soon after riding as possible. Walking around in them should be avoided as it makes them wear out faster. They will last longer and look better if worn only when riding.

Everyone has their own style for polishing boots and their own preference for boot polishes. Therefore, only one method is described here. Wipe dust from your boots with a dry cloth. If there is any dirt stuck on the boots — such as hair or sweat marks on the inside of the leg — use a sponge and warm water to scrub it off.

A small polishing brush or a rag works well for applying polish. Dip the rag or the brush into a small amount of water, then into the polish, and apply it to the boot. Cover the boot except for the inside of the calf. Polish in the calf area will get transferred onto your saddle, horse, and pad, and it is very difficult to clean off. Soon after applying the polish, give the boots a good buffing with your soft-bristled boot brush. Apply another coat of polish and buff again. Take an old pair of stockings and give the boots a final rubbing for a high-gloss sheen.

Put boot trees in your boots to help retain their shape. If you don't have trees, roll up old magazines and insert them in the bootlegs. You can roll up the magazines and secure them with tape, or you can put them inside an old pair of socks and tie the socks securely at the top. Keep trees (or rolled up magazines) in the boots when they are not being worn.

Polishing Spurs

Polish spurs with your favorite metal polish following the manufacturer's instructions. If your straps are leather, clean as advised in the section entitled *Cleaning Leather*. Be sure to clean spur straps frequently to prevent them from cracking and breaking. Nylon spur straps can be cleaned with a damp sponge.

Remove your spurs when you are finished riding. Dirt and debris can become lodged between the spurs and boots, which will scratch the boots and cause them to wear prematurely.

Be Innovative

Although it's nice to have a garment bag, boot bag, hatbox, etc. — and to have them all in your stable colors is even nicer — there are other inexpensive or free solutions to the problem of storing and transporting clothing and equipment. A plastic bag or backpack works well for carrying your bridle, spurs, gloves, and other smaller items. A dry cleaner's bag will adequately protect your coat, breeches, stock tie, and shirt. With a little effort on your part, some plastic bags or cardboard boxes will go far toward maintaining your clothing and equipment in the best possible condition.

Braiding Rubber Bands

Straps — whether cheek pieces, spur straps, or any other — should be tucked neatly into their keepers and runners. If a keeper or runner should break, or the strap is just too long (as is sometimes the case with flash attachments), you can use braiding rubber bands to secure straps. These rubber bands are available at tack shops and come in a variety of colors. Therefore, you won't have any difficulty finding brown, for instance, to match your bridle, or black to match your spur straps. It's good to have a supply of these on hand even if you don't actually use them for braiding.

Learn by Observing

As you walk around the show grounds, take the time to see how other competitors solve their various problems. Look to see how they transport water, store their clothes, set up for the day, and whatever else is of interest to you. There are almost as many solutions as there are competitors. Much can be learned through observation and talking with other competitors and grooms.

Grooming Your Horse for a Show

Now that you've committed to a show, you want to make sure that your horse looks the part. If you have been following a good daily grooming and nutritional program, then preparing for a show won't be too difficult. A thorough and regular grooming program accomplishes several important things:

- It gives you the opportunity to find any injuries your horse may have sustained.
- It increases your horse's blood circulation.
- It improves your horse's looks and overall condition.
- It's a good opportunity to get to know your horse and his preferences.
- It makes him feel good.
- It gives you a chance to check the condition of his hooves and shoes.

Working Efficiently

Because preparing for a show requires a lot of time, there are tasks you can perform several days beforehand so that you aren't rushing at the last minute. For instance, trim the bridlepath, the tail, and fetlocks the weekend before. Last minute touch-ups can be done the night before the show in a matter of minutes.

It's advisable to use a towel when washing your horse's face since towels don't get as sudsy as sponges thereby reducing the chances of accidentally getting soap into your horse's eyes.

Bathing

Giving your horse a soap and water bath is the best way to get him really clean. However, you must consider the climate; you should have a warm, draft-free area in which to bath and dry your horse.

There are plenty of good horse shampoos on the market, so what you use is really a matter of personal preference. If you have a gray horse or a horse with a lot of white in his coat, you should talk to owners of gray horses to see what products they've found work best.

Begin by wetting your horse all over with warm water. Using a hose saves a lot of time if he will tolerate it. Soap him up according to the shampoo instructions, then rinse him thoroughly with clean, warm water and scrape the excess off with your sweat scraper. It is best to wash your horse one section at a time (neck, midsection, hindquarters, legs) and rinse as you go along. This will prevent a build-up of soap that can dull and dry his coat. Be careful to keep soap out of his eyes while washing his face.

Use a coat conditioner such as Show Sheen or Laser Sheen on your horse while he is still damp. After spraying coat conditioner on your horse, work it through with a soft brush to spread it evenly. This gives the coat a nice shine and makes it slippery so that dirt won't stick as easily. Because conditioners do make hair slippery, don't use them in the saddle area or mane. Cover your horse with a cooler after bathing if it's a cool day.

Some people opt to not wash the mane to avoid it being slippery when they braid. Wash and rinse the tail thoroughly and apply a mane and tail detangler so that you don't break any hairs when combing it out. If you are going to braid the tail, do not use de-tanglers in the dock area because this will make it slippery and difficult to braid.

After the Bath

Now that you've put in the time and effort to get your horse spotlessly clean and dazzling, you'll want to keep him that way. Be sure that his stall is immaculate, with plenty of clean bedding. If the weather is not too hot, you can put a clean, lightweight stable sheet on him. Remove soiled bedding from the stall frequently to minimize his chances of getting stains.

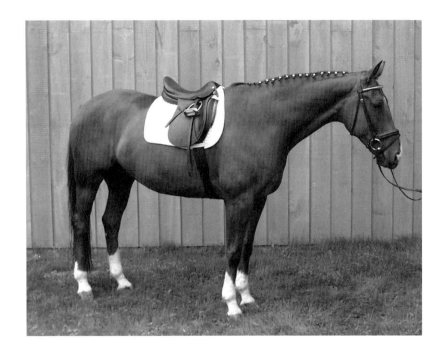

Helenikos is bathed, braided, and well-turned out for a competition. His braids have been done up with white tape, and his tack and saddle pad are clean.

White Socks

If your horse has white legs, wash them thoroughly and wrap them. Otherwise, you can wash them the morning of the show time permitting. It is also useful to clip your horse's legs before washing to improve their appearance. On the day of the show, you can rub corn starch or baby powder into your horse's white stockings to make them their whitest.

Manes

There are a number of ways to prepare your horse's mane for a show. Selecting what to do with his mane will depend on his breed, and on whether you compete in other disciplines in addition to dressage. For instance, it's considered the norm for Norwegian Fjords to have roached manes. Freisians, on the other hand, are noted for their long, flowing manes. Roaching (clipping the entire mane off) is an acceptable alternative for horses that won't tolerate mane pulling or braiding, although it's not one of the more popular solutions to this problem.

Braiding is not mandatory, but if well done, it can enhance the appearance of the horse's neck — and it looks tidier. Many small braids will make

Keeping your horse's mane pulled on a regular basis is less stressful to your horse and easier on you, too, than pulling an overgrown mane all at once.

a neck that is short and thick look longer and more elegant, while fewer braids will complement the horse that has a somewhat long neck. There are different types of braids including, but not limited to, hunter, button, bump, and French.

There are no rules regarding which side of the neck the mane should lie on, so most people braid the mane over to the side where the bulk of it lies naturally. A show-quality braiding job requires two things: (1) a mane that has been pulled properly so that the length and thickness are consistent, and (2) proficiency at braiding. Braiding is a learned skill that comes with extensive practice. For this reason, don't wait until the day before the show to practice braiding — practice on a regular basis well in advance of the show date. This practice will also help you determine which areas of your horse's mane need shortening, thinning, or both.

There are numerous books and magazine articles that provide detailed descriptions on the correct way to braid and the different types of braids. In addition to a good pulling job, it's important to keep the mane very wet while braiding to keep the hairs in place. This can be done with a water brush or by sponging the mane and then combing the water through. You should wet the mane frequently throughout the braiding process so that the hairs stick together.

If you have a very early morning ride, you can braid the night before. However, you may want to practice ahead of time to determine whether your horse is the type who rubs his braids out during the night. If so, plan to get up at least one hour earlier on the morning of the show to braid his mane. As a final touch, some people choose to bind their braids with white tape, which looks nice and helps in keeping stray hairs pinned down.

Tails

Some horses are born with thick, beautiful tails while other horses are not so lucky. No matter what type of tail your horse was born with, it can always be improved through proper grooming and trimming, which will go far towards improving the condition of his tail as well as the appearance.

Whether you choose to use yarn for braiding or to sew in your braids, it's best to use yarn or thread that matches the color of your horse's mane.

Pick hay and shavings out of your horse's tail on a daily basis. In warm weather, wash it regularly and apply a de-tangler. The best way to keep your horse's tail thick and long is to avoid brushing it or using any products that will dry the hair, thereby causing hairs to break more easily. Although it's a time-consuming process, de-tangling your horse's tail by hand is the best method. Start at the bottom of the tail, and separate a few strands at a time. Gradually work your way up the tail in the same fashion. If the hairs catch, do not pull — very carefully separate one hair at a time. Apply a hair conditioner to your horse's tail two to three times a week to help keep it from getting knotted. Avoid products that contain alcohol, as this dries the tail and causes the hair to break more easily.

The tail can be trimmed around the dock, braided, or left au naturel. Some people choose to bang the end of the tail (cut it straight across) for a cleaner appearance. To make the tail look fuller and tidier, you can shape it at the top and bang it at the bottom. Start one to two inches below the point of the buttock, and trim upwards on either side of the dock. You can use scissors or clippers to trim the dock. Trim several weeks before the show and do touch-ups every few days. By trimming several weeks before the show, you give yourself some leeway in case you made a mistake. The hair will have grown back enough to hide all but the most egregious mistakes.

A nicely trimmed tail. Notice that it is shaped in the dock area and banged at the bottom. Photo: Cindy Sydnor

Once the dock area is trimmed, you should bang the end of the tail. Banging is the trimming of the bottom of the tail to make it look tidier and fuller. It is customary to trim the tail to a length about halfway between the hocks and ankles. Although very long tails are quite impressive, there is the risk of the horse stepping on it while getting up after sleeping or rolling, and tearing out a large section.

Stallions forelocks are typically not braided.

Be sure to wash your brushes on a regular basis. Warm water and mild soap work well. For leather-backed brushes, you can add Murphy's Oil Soap to the wash water. Dry off the leather handle with a towel and apply a light coating of oil.

This is why most people opt to trim the tail to ankle length. If a friend is available to help, have the friend hold their arm under the horse's dock to lift the tail up and away from your horse's body. Otherwise, roll up a towel so that it is the size of a person's arm, and place it under your horse's dock. Another method for determining where to bang the tail is to make the bottom of the tail even with the top of the windpuff area. If your horse has a naturally high tail carriage, you may want to leave it a bit longer.

When you trim the end of the tail, angle it slightly from front to back. This will make the tail appear as though it's trimmed straight across when the horse is working under saddle.

Finally, although braiding of the tail was previously seen only in the hunter rings in the U.S., it is gaining popularity among dressage competitors in Europe and will probably become popular here as well. If you are a trendsetter who is adept at braiding tails, this is another method for making the tail look nice for a show.

Cold Weather Bathing

Early spring shows and fall shows sometimes entail cold weather. You don't want to risk having your horse get chilled and sick, but you still want him to be clean for the show. Without actually bathing the horse, you can still get him clean by using hot water and towels.

Keep a cooler on him throughout the process and keep him out of any drafts. Roll the cooler from his poll to his withers, then soak a towel in comfortably hot water, wring it out, and rub his neck area briskly in a circular motion as though you are currying. When through, roll the cooler forward, and give the towel a good rinse. Fold the cooler from his tail to his hips and clean his hindquarters with the damp towel. Move back to his forehand and clean the shoulder and saddle area. Moving from front to back to midsection gives each area a few minutes in which to dry.

Rub him with a dry towel to speed the drying process. Depending on the temperature, you may want to use just a wool cooler or a wool cooler on top of an Irish knit. The important thing is to keep your horse covered and out of any drafts.

Dressing the Hooves

Some people choose to apply oil to their horse's feet or use hoof polish, which comes in either clear or black. If you choose to oil or polish your horse's feet, be sure to do so on a wooden floor, paved floor, or grass. Wait until his hooves are dry before walking him on dirt, into a stall, or on any other surface material that can stick to his feet.

If using oil, keep it away from the nail holes in your horse's hooves as oil softens the feet making the nails less secure.

Trimming

It is customary to trim ears, the bridlepath and throat latch areas, and the fetlocks; however, hairs around the horse's eyes and muzzle should be left alone because horses use these hairs as feelers to avoid bumping into things. When trimming the bridlepath area, trim it so that it is approximately 1/4 inch wider than the crown piece of your bridle.

Although some people trim the inside of their horse's ears, it is best not to since this leaves the horse with no protection against bugs in the summer and cold in the winter. A more popular type of ear trimming is to gently squeeze the ear together and use scissors or ear clippers to trim hairs that protrude from the ears. This creates a tidy appearance around the edges of the ears without depriving the horse of much needed protection from the elements.

Dressing Your Horse for a Show

For Introductory through Third levels, competitors are required to compete in a snaffle bridle. The bits and nosebands legal for this level of competition are as follows:

Bits

The AHSA (*Article 1921 — Saddlery and Equipment*) states that the following bits are legal.

- Ordinary snaffle with single-jointed mouthpiece.
- Ordinary snaffle with double-jointed mouthpiece.
- Racing snaffle (Dee-ring).
- Other Ordinary snaffle — a) with cheeks, with or without keepers; b) without cheeks (egg butt).
- Snaffle with upper or lower cheeks.
- Unjointed snaffle (Mullen-mouth).
- Snaffle with cheeks (hanging or drop cheek; Baucher). This may be a D-ring or snaffle.
- Dr. Bristol.
- Fulmer.
- French snaffle.

Helenikos is wearing a snaffle bridle with a loose ring snaffle bit and cavesson with a flash attachment. This bridle is acceptable for Introductory through Fourth levels. Competitors at Fourth level have the option of using a double bridle. FEI level riders must use a double bridle.

This is a brown bridle with a decorative silver browband Brown or black tack is acceptable, and the nosebands can be self-padded or have white padding. Ideally, this noseband should be 1/2" - 1" higher on "Nicky's" face.

These bits can be covered with rubber or leather, and mouthpieces of synthetic material are allowed, provided that the contours of the material conform to the contours of the bit. Bits must be smooth with a solid surface; twisted, wire, and roller bits are illegal. The mouthpiece may be made of two different metals.

Nosebands

Nosebands must be made of leather or a leather-like material and may be padded. The following nosebands are permitted for use with snaffle bridles:

- Regular cavesson.
- Dropped noseband.
- Flash noseband (this is a regular cavesson with a flash attachment; a strap that acts in the same way as a dropped noseband. This noseband may not be adjusted so tightly that it causes skin irritation).

- Padded noseband.
- Crescent noseband or a crossed noseband.

Saddles

The AHSA states that the saddle must be an English type saddle with stirrups. The leather color (black or brown) does not matter, nor does it matter if the saddle is an all-purpose, jumping, or dressage saddle. What *does* matter, to you and your horse, is that it fits you both properly.

Saddle Pads

Although there are no set rules regarding saddle pads, most riders prefer square, white pads. Square or swallow tail pads are strongly advised for upper level riders as they help keep tailcoat tails from collecting sweat or dirt from the horse. Plain white pads are predominant. Less common are black pads with black or white borders, or white pads with colored borders.

Saddle pad shape, color, and size are a matter of personal preference. However, if you are wearing a cream-colored shirt, stock tie, breeches, and gloves, it is nice to color coordinate by using a cream-colored saddle pad.

When selecting a saddle pad, consider the length of your horse's back. If he is somewhat short in the back, avoid large pads; however, if he's long in the back, a large pad will be more flattering.

Breed logos and sponsor's logos (as shown in picture at left) are permitted on saddle pads. Photo: Mary Phelps

Fourth level tests may be ridden in either a snaffle or a double bridle as long as the bits meet the AHSA's rules. Fourth level riders using a double bridle must wear a short jacket rather than a tailcoat.

Numbers

Numbers are assigned to each horse and given to competitors when they pick up their show packets upon arriving at the show grounds. The number(s) must be worn at all times when a horse is being exercised or ridden.

If you lose your number, report the loss to the show secretary immediately. Riding without a number can result in elimination.

If you are given two numbers, put one on either side of your browband. If you are given just one number, place it on the left side of your browband. Some horses do not take kindly to having numbers attached to their browbands. If this is the case with your horse, attach your number to the outside of your boot top.

Illegal Equipment

Equipment that is illegal in the competition ring as well as the warm-up and training areas includes:

- Bit guards.
- Any gadget (bearing, running, balancing reins, tongue tied down, etc.).
- Any form of blinkers.
- Ear muffs.
- Ear plugs.
- Seat covers for the saddle.
- Hoods (strictly forbidden!).
- Decorations on the horse (flowers, ribbons, etc.).
- Long lining (similar to longeing but with a longe line attached on either side) is not permitted.

Equipment that May Be Used *ONLY* in Warm-Up or Training Areas

- Running martingales (with snaffle only).
- Single direct side reins are permitted but only when longeing a horse.
- Exercise horse boots (this includes "easy boots").
- Bandages (leg or tail). Leg bandages are permitted in Pas de Deux.
- Nose covers.
- Standard longeing whip.
- Two whips no longer than 6' including the lash.
- Horses at Fourth level or above may warm up in a snaffle.

Equipment for FEI Levels

The Double Bridle

Fourth level tests may be ridden in a snaffle or a double bridle. All FEI level tests are ridden in a double bridle. The double bridle has two bits (a snaffle and a curb) and two reins, hence its name. The snaffle bit that is used on a double bridle is called a bridoon and is smaller than the snaffle bit that you would typically use on a snaffle bridle — the bridoon rings are smaller and the mouthpiece is usually thinner.

Types of Bridoons (snaffles):

- Ordinary bridoon bit.
- Bridoon bit with two joints.
- Egg butt bridoon bit.
- Bridoon bit with cheeks or drop and cheek bridoon
- Note: The D-ring bridoon (or racing snaffle) is not permitted as part of a double bridle.

Types of Curbs:

- Half-moon curb bit.
- Curb bit with straight cheeks and port.
- Curb bit with port and sliding mouthpiece (Weymouth).
- Variation of curb bit with straight cheeks and port.
- Curb bit with s-curved cheeks.

Other:

- Curb chain (this may be covered with leather or rubber).
- Lip strap.

Bit measurements:

The lever arm of the curb cannot exceed 10 cm, and the ring of the bridoon of a double bridle must not exceed 8 cm in diameter.

Dressing the Rider for a Show

Dressing for competition is dependent upon the level at which you are competing. Correct attire for AHSA recognized competitions is shown in the table at the end of this chapter.

Special Exceptions to the Dress Code

In excessively hot (above 85 degrees) or humid conditions, show management may allow riders to show without jackets. When showing without a jacket, wear a white or pale-colored shirt with long or short sleeves, and remove your neckwear, but leave the shirt buttoned at the collar. Hats are mandatory, and T-shirts and sleeveless shirts are specifically prohibited.

In rainy weather, riders may wear a hat cover and a raincoat that is transparent or conservative in color.

Hair

Unless you have extremely short hair, you will need to tie it back, and you should also use a hair net to prevent wisps of hair from sticking out. You will want to experiment at home with various hairstyles to find one that looks nice but doesn't interfere with the proper fit of your headgear.

Candi Piscopo is appropriately attired for Introductory through Fourth levels. Her clothing is a good fit and obviously well cared for. Candi is holding a snaffle bridle with a crank noseband and flash attachment. The bit is a loose ring French link snaffle. This bit and bridle are legal for competition at Introductory through Fourth levels.

Although gloves are optional until the FEI levels, they do create a more polished look. White or light tan gloves are traditional and elegant.

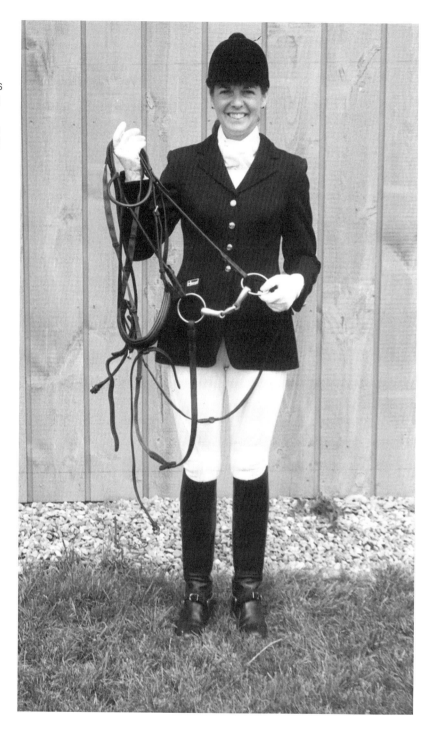

Riding Boots

At the FEI levels, black boots are specified. At the lower levels, brown or black are permitted, but black is customary. Most people choose black leather dress boots, but there is no rule that prohibits riders from wearing rubber boots, field boots, or boots with zippers. Although black dress boots are the norm, zippered boots and field boots (which have the lacing along the front of the ankle) are good choices for riders with particularly high insteps or conformation that make regular boots difficult to fit. Placement of the zippers — along the back seam or on the inside of the calf — is strictly a matter of personal preference.

Logos

Logos are permitted. A logo not exceeding 80 square cm. in size may be worn on the breast pocket of the rider's jacket. Logos of 16 square cm. or less are permitted on shirt collars.

Dress Code for FEI Junior Tests

Correct attire for juniors riding FEI Tests is a short riding coat of conservative color with stock or tie, breeches, hunt cap or riding hat with a hard shell, derby or top hat. Spurs are mandatory for all of the FEI Junior Tests.

Introductory Level Attire

Because Introductory level is not a level recognized by the AHSA, there are no written rules for attire at this level. However, you can't go wrong if you adhere to the rules for Training through Fourth levels as set forth in the table at the end of this chapter.

A Note on Hats

If wearing protective headgear with a harness, a clear harness is preferable. Velvet hunt caps and bowlers are typical choices for the lower levels, while top hats are required at the FEI levels for riders wearing tailcoats.

Dressing for a Schooling Show

Although most schooling shows adhere to AHSA rules, there is typically more leniency in rider attire than at recognized shows. If you have any concerns

Susan Russell is correctly attired for the FEI levels (Prix St Georges, Intermediaire I and II, and Grand Prix). It is appropriate to wear a top hat when wearing a shadbelly coat as shown here.

Susan is holding a double bridle, which is required at the FEI levels. Double bridles get their name because they have two bits: a snaffle (bridoon) and a curb.

about your attire, contact the show manager or show secretary for clarification. No matter what you choose to wear, be sure that it is well-fitting, clean, and comfortable.

The Dress Code As Set Forth by the AHSA

Clothing	Training-Fourth Levels	FEI Levels
Boots	Boots or jodphur boots	Black boots
Breeches	Breeches or jodphurs	White or light colored breeches
Coat	Short coat of conservative color	Dark tailcoat or dark jacket
Gloves	Optional	Mandatory.
Half Chaps and Leggings	Not permitted	Not permitted
Hat	Hunt cap or riding hat with hard shell, derby, or top hat. ASTM approved helmets are permitted	Top hat if wearing a tailcoat, and bowler (derby) if wearing a short jacket. Protective headgear may be worn with tailcoat or short jacket
Neckwear	Tie, choker, or hunting stock	Hunting stock or tie
Shirt	White or light-colored shirt with long or short sleeves. T-shirts are prohibited	Same
Spurs*	Optional	Mandatory
Whips	Must not be longer than 4' including the lash. Whips are not allowed in AHSA/USDF championship classes, USET Championships, USET Qualifying and Selection Trials, or Observation classes. However, sidesaddle riders may carry a whip in any test.	Same

* Spurs must be made of metal, and there must be a shank, either curved or straight, pointing directly back from the center of the spur. If the shank is curved, the spurs must be worn only with the shank directed downwards. However, swan necked spurs are allowed. The arms of the spur must be smooth. If rowels are used, they must be free to rotate. This restriction also applies to warm-up and training areas, as well as during competition. *(AHSA, 1998-1999 Dressage Division Rulebook, Article 1920, #8)*

The Dressage Arena

There are two sizes of dressage arena:

- The small arena, which measures 20 meters by 40 meters (66 feet by 132 feet).
- The standard arena, which measures 20 meters by 60 meters (66 feet by 198 feet).

Typically, the small arena is used for Introductory and Training levels, and the standard arena is used for First level through Grand Prix. However, Training level tests are occasionally held in a standard arena. For this reason, Training level competitors should practice riding in a standard arena so that they know exactly where their 20-meter circles should be. See *Appendix E* for detailed diagrams of arenas and the placement of the various sized circles.

Building Your Own Arena

If you keep your horse at home and have land on which to build an arena, you should contact the USDF for a copy of their booklet entitled *Under Foot: The USDF Guide to Dressage Arena Construction, Maintenance,*

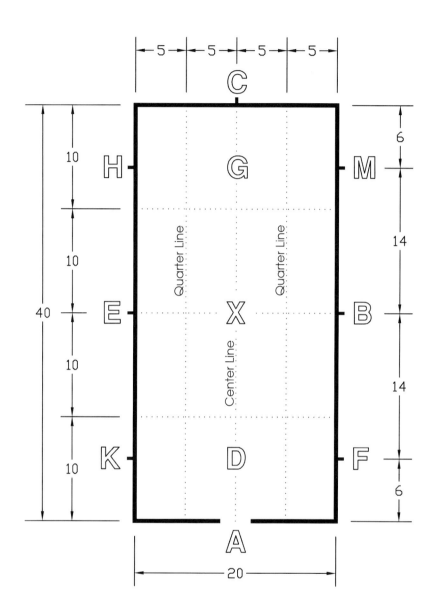

The Small Arena — 20 m x 40 m

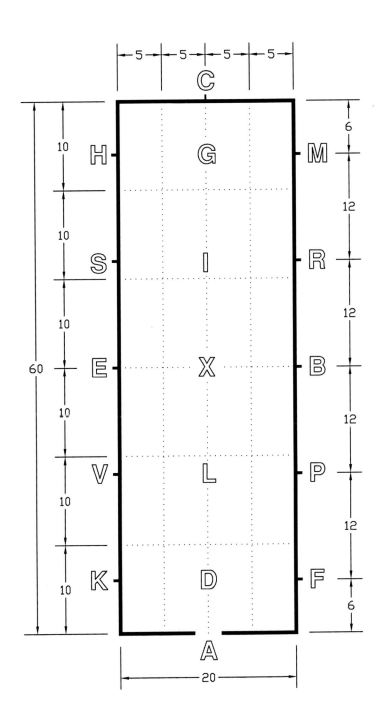

All dimensions are in meters.

1 meter	3.28 feet
6 meters	19.69 feet
10 meters	32.81 feet
12 meters	39.37 feet
14m eters	45.93 feet
20 meters	65.62 feet
40 meters	131.24 feet
60 meters	196.86 feet

The Standard Arena — 20 m x 60 m

and Repair. This manual describes the different types of footing materials, the various drainage methods, and the numerous other details that go into building an arena.

Improvising

If you are one of the many people who don't have enough land on which to build a regulation size dressage arena, and you are too far away from one to get there by hacking or even trailering, don't despair. This is where your resourcefulness comes into play. Find a section of your property that is as level as possible and prepare it by removing trees, saplings, stones, and any other footing hazards. Fill in holes, and mow if needed. Even if you can't get exact dressage arena dimensions, do your best to have a width of at least 60 feet and a length of at least 100 feet. Every year, set aside some time and/or money for improving your ring. In the first year, you may want to invest in getting a bulldozer in to level it. Another year, you may want to concentrate on improving the drainage and footing.

Once you have cleared an area where you can practice, there are a number of inexpensive methods for putting up markers — limited only by your imagination. One of the simplest methods is to get plastic one-gallon milk jugs, fill them with sand so that they won't blow over in the wind, and use a waterproof magic marker to write letters on them. It's not an elegant solution, but it serves its purpose. It really doesn't matter how you make the markers since there are just two things you are trying to accomplish in having them: 1) to practice being more precise in your transitions, and 2) to get your horse accustomed to markers. Horses that have never competed are apt to spook at the white arena and letters. If they've already seen markers at home, they are less apt to be distracted by them at a show.

Measuring Your Arena

If you have enough land on which to build either a small or a standard arena, follow these steps to make sure that it is straight and that it has the correct dimensions:

1) Set two corner markers 20 meters (66 feet) apart, which is the arena width for small and standard size arenas.

2) Start at the left corner marker, and measure off a length of 132 feet if

building a small arena, and 198 feet if building a standard arena. Do the same from the right corner marker.

3) To ensure that the arena is straight, use the Pythagorean Theorem. (This is accomplished by adding your short side squared to your long side squared and taking the square root of the total.) According to this theorem, the distance from your near left corner to your far right corner and from your near right corner to your far left corner should be 147'7" for a small arena and 208'8" for a standard arena.

4) Assemble your white plastic chain border (or whatever fencing material you choose), and enclose your ring.

5) Now you can begin placing your markers around the arena.

6) Place markers one-half to one meter away from the arena border.

Arrangement of the Letters

As shown in the diagrams at the beginning of this chapter, letters are placed at strategic points around the arena. **A** is always where you enter and **C** is where the judge sits — until you reach the higher levels in which case you have judges seated at the quarterlines to either side of **C** and also at **B** or **E**.

Maintaining Your Arena

You will want to keep the surface of your arena smooth and the footing material evenly distributed. The ring should not be excessively deep nor excessively hard. Hard surfaces are stressful to a horse's joints while surfaces that are too soft are stressful to soft tissue and ligaments. You will need to drag your arena based on how often it is used and by how many horses. Obviously, arenas that are used by a number of riders on a daily basis will have to be dragged daily. If you are riding one horse per day in your arena, you can get away with less frequent dragging. Equipment for dragging an arena can be as elaborate as a tractor with a harrow attached to it or a small car or garden tractor with a small harrow. A cheap solution to a harrow is an old bedspring (available from your local landfill at no charge) that is weighted with a couple of cement blocks.

If the footing in your arena tends to get packed down and hard, drag it at a low speed. This allows the teeth of the harrow to dig into the earth and loosen it up. Driving too fast will cause the harrow to bounce across the top of the surface, and the ground will not be loosened as effectively. You will

An easy way to remember the arrangement of the letters around a small arena is this (origin unknown) — starting at A and moving clockwise — **A**ll **K**ind **E**lephants **H**ave **C**ommon **M**others **B**rothers **F**athers.

want a hose with a sprinkler that can reach your arena so that you can water it as needed to keep the dust down.

Deciding What Level to Enter

Your instructor is the best person to consult regarding what level you should enter; however, if you don't have a regular instructor, there are a number of other methods for determining the appropriate level for you and your horse.

Several things to consider are:

- The type of work you and your horse are proficient at while riding at home.
- Your horse's previous show experience (if any).
- Your previous show experience (if any).
- Your horse's behavior when introduced into a new setting.
- Your poise in a competition setting.

Compete at One Level Lower

It's common for experienced riders to compete at one level lower than that at which they are schooling. For instance, a rider who is schooling all of the Second level movements at home would most likely compete at First level. If you are working on walk, trot, and canter at home and are new to cantering, you would be well advised to enter one or both of the Introductory level tests, which don't require any cantering.

You may enter more than one level with the same horse. However, the levels must be contiguous. For instance, you can enter Training and First levels or Second and Third, but you cannot enter Training and Second, First and Fourth, and so on.

Choosing Specific Tests

In addition to being able to select a level, you can also pick and choose which tests from that level you want to ride. Read through all the tests within that level and select the test(s) that best showcases your horse's and your skills. If you have decided on Training level but aren't overly confident about your sitting trot, you could choose to enter Test 1, Test 2, or both since the trot work can be performed at the rising or the sitting trot. Tests 3 and 4, on the other hand, specifically call for sitting trot for most of the trot work.

As another example, First level has 4 tests with Test 1 being the most basic and Test 4 the most difficult. If your horse is a solid First level horse schooling most of the Second level movements, but he is not confirmed in the counter canter, you could choose to ride First level Tests 1, 2, or 3 and skip 4 which includes two counter canter loops.

Spectate, Scribe, Ride in a Clinic, and Videotape

Other methods for determining what level to enter include:

* Spectating at shows so that you can see riders performing the tests that you are considering entering.
* Volunteering to scribe at a show. Sitting next to a judge and hearing her comments firsthand will give you a good understanding of what is expected by the judge at a particular level.
* Riding in a clinic and asking the clinician's opinion.
* Having someone videotape you so that you can see how your horse and you actually look.

Spectate

Spectating at a show where you plan to compete is fun and educational. Spectating also gives you the opportunity to become familiar with the show grounds before actually competing there. You can locate the arenas, warm-up area, water source, parking, restrooms, scoreboards, concession stands, etc. before you compete so that when you do arrive at the show as a competitor, you'll know the location of everything and feel right at home. Spectating also provides an opportunity for you to meet and talk with competitors, grooms, and non-competing riders. Much can be learned by listening to and participating in conversations with these people.

School Your Horse at the Show Grounds

Some show grounds are owned by clubs that permit their members to use the facility for schooling when a competition isn't being held. Some clubs permit non-members use of their facilities if the non-member agrees to pay a fee and sign a release form. This can be a wonderful schooling opportunity for first-time competitors. If you haven't trailered your horse before, this is also a good opportunity to find out how he loads and rides in the trailer without your feeling pressured by time constraints.

Scribe

Scribing is another means for getting a really good education (gratis) while you simultaneously do a good deed by helping out the organizers of a competition. As a scribe, you will sit next to the judge and record her comments and scores for every ride she judges. Some shows will provide you with a list of dressage shorthand symbols, which makes it easier for you to keep up with a judge's comments. The USDF publishes a pamphlet entitled *Guide for Dressage Competition Scribes* that has a list of shorthand symbols and clearly explains what is expected of a scribe.

Judges are grateful to have conscientious scribes and will reward your efforts by conveying useful information to you during the course of your scribing. Should you volunteer to scribe, be sure to be well prepared: wear clothing appropriate for the weather, carry sunblock with you in the summer, plenty of cold (or hot) drinks, food, and a good supply of pencils with erasers and a pencil sharpener. Some shows provide food and pencils, but it's always good to bring your own just in case.

Ride in a Clinic

The obvious benefit to riding in a clinic is the knowledge you will acquire; a new set of eyes may uncover something that has slipped your regular instructor's notice. It's also an excellent opportunity to take your horse to a new and different facility.

Clinicians commonly use the first few minutes of each lesson to ask you about yourself, your horse, and the areas in which you think you need help. They will frequently save a few minutes at the end to answer any questions you may have. At the beginning of the lesson, tell the clinician that you are

While spectating, you will undoubtedly notice that some riders stand out from the crowd. These are the people to whom you will want to pay special attention. You can learn much by watching carefully to see what it is that sets them apart from everyone else.

planning on entering your first show, and that you would appreciate his opinion on the level you should enter. Experienced clinicians can usually determine during the course of the lesson what's appropriate for you.

To make the most of a clinic situation, prepare for it the way you would a show. You can even braid your horse's mane if you like. Groom your horse, clean your tack, and prepare your clothing and everything else as though you were headed for a competition. Not only will it make you aware of areas that may need improvement, but it will give you an idea as to the amount of time and work involved in getting ready for a competition. When the "real" thing comes around, you'll feel more prepared and probably more relaxed.

Videotape

If you are fortunate enough to have a video camera, or access to one, ask someone to videotape you riding. If your instruction is infrequent because of finances or distance from your trainer, you can probably make arrangements to mail the tape to her for review. This is particularly useful if your instructor has not seen you and your horse for several months.

Deciding the Number of Tests to Ride

By now, you are probably wondering how many tests to enter. It is common at the lower levels to ride two tests per day. Three isn't unheard of, but can be quite tiring for horse and rider.

At the FEI levels, riders typically ride one test per day because the tests are so demanding.

Entering a Competition

Entering a competition requires planning. You must have copies of all the appropriate paperwork, and you must complete the entry form carefully.

When you enter any competition, you must have a current Coggins test. This test verifies that your horse has tested negative for Equine Infectious Anemia (EIA). Most shows are satisfied with a Coggins test that is dated within one year of the competition date, but some shows require that it be dated within the last six months. Read the prize list carefully to find this information. Some shows may require other documentation such as a health certificate dated within 10 days of the show and/or a Rabies certificate. Refer to the prize list or Omnibus to learn what certificates are required by the show you are entering.

If you are pursuing AHSA, USDF, breed, or other year-end awards, you will need current membership for yourself and your horse in those organizations. In most cases, the horse's owner (if other than you) must also be a current member of these organizations. Make several photocopies of your membership cards, and store the originals in a safe place.

Depending on where you plan to compete, you may want to have your horse vaccinated for Potomac Horse Fever.

Transporting Horses Interstate

In the event that you plan to compete out of state, you must be aware of any local, county, or state regulations regarding transporting horses interstate. Some states require specific immunizations or health certificates. Typically, you must have a health certificate for your horse that is dated within 10 days of your travel date in order to cross state borders.

You must also be aware of vehicle weight regulations and the type of driver's license required to drive a horse van. Additionally, trucks and trailers are not permitted on some highways. Be sure to check your route carefully before leaving home to avoid time-consuming reroutings.

American Horse Council
1700 K Street NW, Suite 700
Washington, DC 20006
Tel. 202-296-4031

For information on each state's health certificate requirements, contact the American Horse Council, and request a copy of their *Directory*.

The Prize List

The prize list is the document containing all the information you need to enter a particular show. It includes the show date, location, names of judges, levels and tests offered, awards, opening and closing dates, rules and regulations, fees, footing in arenas as well as warm up areas, and more. The prize list will include an entry form. Schooling shows as well as some of the larger shows have their own prize lists that they send to their members or anyone else who requests a copy.

The Omnibus

Some of the recognized shows send out their own prize lists rather than being listed in the Omnibus.

The Omnibus is a book that lists all of the AHSA/USDF recognized shows in a particular region. There are nine AHSA regions and nine USDF regions. Refer to *Appendix B* for a listing of states that are included in each USDF region. The Omnibus contains all of the information that a prize list contains with the shows listed in chronological order. Two official generic entry forms are included in this book, and competitors are responsible for making enough photocopies to get them through the show season.

Omnibuses are available for all nine USDF regions.

Competitions listed in the Omnibus provide more information than schooling show prize lists since many people will be traveling further and will need overnight accommodations. In addition to the information provided in a schooling show prize list, the Omnibus prize list also includes hotels with their phone numbers and their distance from the show grounds, information about food concessions on the show grounds, information on stabling, and driving directions.

Opening and Closing Dates

The opening date is the earliest date that the envelope containing your entry form can be postmarked, and the closing date is the latest date that the envelope containing your entry form can be postmarked. Closing dates are set well in advance of the competition date because it's a significant logistical task for show secretaries to schedule rides. Therefore, it's a good idea to be aware of the opening and closing dates and to mail your entry form on the opening date.

Refunds

Most shows will refund your entry fee less an office fee if your horse is sick or injured and you submit a veterinarian's certificate *before* the closing date. No refunds are given after the closing date. The prize list or Omnibus provides information on each show's policy regarding refunds.

Post Entering

Occasionally, it's possible to post enter — enter after the closing date — if the show has not filled. There is also the possibility of post entering if someone scratches (withdraws) from a test that you want to enter. However, there is usually an additional fee for post entering. The prize list or Omnibus provides specific information for each show.

Ride Times

Approximately one week before the show, the show secretary sends competitors a postcard with their ride times. Printed on this card are the tests you entered and the times that you will be riding them. Some shows will even include the arena in which your test will be held and the judge's name. Check the prize list to see if you are required to send a self-addressed stamped envelope in order to get this information. Some shows do require an SASE.

Completing the Entry Form

Entry forms for schooling shows are simpler than those for AHSA/USDF sanctioned shows. Nonetheless, you must be equally diligent when completing either one. Incomplete, incorrect, or entries without proper payment are usually put at the bottom of the pile and dealt with last. This isn't because show secretaries are inherently "evil" people; on the contrary, they work hard to keep things running smoothly. However, because they receive numerous entries, they would get bogged down if they stopped and dealt with each incorrect entry as it arrived. Therefore, secretaries handle the correct entries first and then proceed to the others. If yours is one of "the others," you run the risk of being put on the waiting list if the show fills. This could mean that you don't get in at all.

When you are completing your entry form, don't forget:

- Fill the form out completely.
- Sign your name wherever indicated. If you are under 21 years of age, a parent or guardian must sign.
- Be sure to calculate fees properly, and make the check payable to whomever the prize list indicates.
- If the prize list indicates that you need to make out a separate check for the number deposit or a stall cleaning fee (if you are renting a stall), be sure to make out a separate check. These fees are refunded at the end of the show when you return your number(s) and clean your stall.
- Be sure that your entry is postmarked on or after the opening date and on or before the closing date.
- Include a copy of your horse's current negative Coggins test.
- Include copies of any other health certificates required such as Rabies, Potomac Horse Fever, current health certificate, etc.
- Include copies of your AHSA and USDF membership cards.
- Include copies of your horse's AHSA and USDF registration cards.

The Entry Form for Recognized Shows

The entry form for USDF/AHSA recognized shows is more comprehensive than that for schooling shows because a number of competitors at these shows are pursuing year-end awards. To be eligible for most awards, riders and owners must be members of the USDF, the AHSA, or both and, in some cases, their horses must be registered with the USDF, the AHSA, or both. See

Two copies of the OPL (Omnibus Prize List) entry form are included with the Omnibus. It is the competitor's responsibility to make additional copies of these entry forms.

the chapters entitled *Memberships* and *Awards Programs* for detailed membership and awards program information.

The OPL Entry Form is used for all AHSA/USDF recognized shows nationwide and is mostly self-explanatory. Be sure to make an adequate number of photocopies of this form. Only one horse may be entered on each entry form. If you are competing more than one horse, include copies of your membership cards with each entry; don't put the show secretary in the position of having to match up membership cards with entry forms.

Basic information such as the name, address, and phone number of the rider is entered at the top of the form as well as the horse's owner's name and the trainer's name if you have a trainer. The horse's name, age, breed, sex, height, etc. must be entered. The top third of the front side of the form is straightforward and won't cause any hair pulling. The middle section is not necessarily as straightforward and is explained in more detail below.

Enter your AHSA and USDF membership numbers and those of the owner and trainer. If the owner and trainer are you, enter your own number in these blocks. See the chapter entitled *Memberships* for an in depth discussion of the different types of memberships and what is required to participate in the various awards programs.

[Note: Italicized text in the sections below indicates actual headings on the OPL entry form.]

AHSA/USDF Member Numbers

The section of the entry form that requests USDF/AHSA numbers can cause some confusion. The following is clarification of this section so that you won't have your entry form put at the bottom of the show secretary's stack of entries.

USDF Numbers

Indicate any current numbers — Enter your USDF number in the Rider block. If you are the owner and trainer, enter your USDF number in these blocks as well. Otherwise, enter the owner's and trainer's numbers as appropriate. In order to qualify for any USDF awards, other than rider awards, your horse must be registered with the USDF. Enter your horse's USDF reg-

You must enter a name in the *Horse's Name* block on the entry form. Management is not permitted to accept entries that read "not named."

istration number in the appropriate block. [Note: your horse does not have to be registered with any organization for you to participate in rider awards, but *you* must be a USDF member].

AHSA Numbers

Indicate membership number — Enter AHSA membership numbers in the appropriate blocks: *rider, owner, trainer, and horse.*

Indicate copy AHSA card enclosed — Check the appropriate box(es) to indicate that you are an AHSA member and are enclosing a copy of your membership card. Don't forget to enclose a photocopy of your membership card as well as photocopies of the membership cards of the owner and trainer if other than you!

Senior members — pay $5 Br/Disc fee if required — This is a breed/discipline fee. If you are not an AHSA member, you will be required to pay a $5 breed/discipline fee. If you are an AHSA member, disregard this fee.

Pay $5 Affidavit fee if no card copy — If your AHSA membership is pending (that is, you have applied for membership but not yet received your card), enter $5 under the appropriate heading. You will be required to pay this affidavit fee until your card comes through and you are able to enclose a photocopy of it with your entry.

Each non-1999 AHSA member: Pay $20 ($15 non member + $5 Br/Disc fee) — If you are not an AHSA member, you are required to pay a $15 non-member fee plus the $5 breed/discipline fee. If you are planning on participating in the AHSA year-end awards program, you must join the AHSA. If you are not planning on participating, but will be competing in three or more shows in one season, you will save money by joining the AHSA rather than paying this $20 fee for each show. In addition, by joining the AHSA you will receive all of the AHSA's rulebooks and *Horse Show* magazine, which will enable you to keep up with any rule changes that may affect you. Non-members who have access to the Internet can look up AHSA rules and rule changes by visiting the AHSA's web site: http://www.ahsa.org and clicking *Rule Book.*

Payment Must Be Included with Entry

This section of the entry form lists all of the fees. Be sure to complete this section carefully and total the figures accurately.

Total of Class Entry Fees — Enter the total of your class fees taken from the *Classes Entered* section to the left.

AHSA/Drugs Medication Fee — This is a mandatory fee, and the amount due is preprinted on the entry form.

Total of AHSA Fees for Rider, Trainer, and Owner — This fee is charged if you are not an AHSA member. For instance, if you are the rider, trainer, and owner and not an AHSA member, you will have to pay the non-AHSA member fee. If neither the rider, trainer, nor owner is an AHSA member, all three will have to pay the non-AHSA member fee.

Office Fee — Check the Omnibus for information on any office fees for which you may be liable. Enter the specified amount (if any) in this space.

Number Deposit — Check the Omnibus to see if a number deposit is required for the show you are entering. If none is required, leave this space blank. Otherwise, enter the amount indicated.

Total of Stabling Fees — Stabling fee information is included in the Omnibus. Enter the amount specified in this space. Some shows require that stabling fees be paid with a separate check.

Non-Compete Horse Fee — Check each individual show's rules to see if they permit non-competing horses. These are horses that riders want to bring to the show for experience but do not intend to compete. If allowed, there is sometimes a fee. Check the Omnibus for this information.

Penalty Fees and Post Entry Fees — Refer to the Omnibus for information on penalty and post entry fees specific to the show you are entering.

TOTAL PAID WITH ENTRY — Total up the fees (excluding the stabling fee) and enter in this space. Make out a check for the total amount made payable to whomever is indicated in the Omnibus.

Stabling Details — The stabling details section of the entry form is self-explanatory. Under the "Special Requests" section, you may, for ex-

If the owner, trainer, or rider is a junior, a parent or guardian must sign the entry form. Although this adult is exempt from the AHSA non-member fee, the minor is not. He/she must be an AHSA member or else pay the non-member fee.

There is no overemphasizing the importance of signing all three signature blocks even if you are the rider, owner, and trainer.

ample, request to be stabled next to your trainer, a friend, or other.

Compulsory Signatures — On the back of the entry form is a block entitled *Compulsory Signatures*. There are spaces for the rider, trainer, and owner. Even if you are the rider, trainer, and owner, you must sign your name in all three places. Do not sign your name in the first block and write "same" underneath. Your entry will not be accepted. Also, note that if you list a trainer, that person is required to be on the show grounds during the competition.

Qualification Information — Complete this section only if you are entering a Championship competition or USDF Regional Final. This is where you record the show, date, level, and percentage score you received in a qualifying class which entitles you to compete in a Championship or Final. See the chapter entitled *Awards Programs* for information on championship and qualifying classes.

Information for Announcer — This information is optional and could include some of your horse's competition highlights, for instance.

Volunteer Information — Complete this section if you are available to help at the show or in the planning stages. Indicate the areas in which you might be interested in helping: scoring, scribing, gatekeeping, etc.

Entry Form Checklist

Before you seal the envelope and mail your entry to the show secretary, be sure that:

- ☑ All three signature blocks are signed.
- ☑ Fees have been totaled correctly.
- ☑ A check for the entry fees is enclosed and you have included the number fee (if required), the office fee (if required), and the stabling fee if you are renting a stall.
- ☑ A separate stall cleaning check is enclosed if you are renting a stall.
- ☑ All AHSA/USDF numbers (horse, rider, owner) are recorded correctly on the entry form.
- ☑ A copy of your AHSA member card is enclosed.

☑ A copy of your USDF member card is enclosed.

☑ A copy of your trainer's AHSA member card is enclosed if you are listing a trainer.

☑ A copy of your trainer's USDF member card is enclosed if you are listing a trainer.

☑ A copy of the owner's AHSA member card if the owner is someone other than you.

☑ A copy of the owner's USDF member card if the owner is someone other than you.

☑ A copy of your horse's AHSA registration is enclosed.

☑ A copy of your horse's USDF registration is enclosed.

☑ A copy of your horse's negative Coggins test is enclosed.

☑ A copy of your horse's Rabies or health certificate is enclosed (if required).

☑ You have included information regarding the competitions where you qualified if you are entering a Championship competition or a USDF Regional Final.

Special Requests

Show managers are typically very accommodating as long as you make your needs known in advance. If you have any special needs, such as some of the following, include a note with your entry.

- Stallion owners — let the show manager know if you have any special stabling requirements. You may either be stabled in a separate barn or be assigned a corner stall. The manager will be able to tell you what's available.
- Stabling with trainer — on the stabling form, you can ask to be stabled in the same stable block as your trainer.
- Riding more than one horse — specify the number of horses you are riding. The person scheduling rides will do their utmost to make sure that you don't encounter any scheduling conflicts.

Packing for and Arriving at the Show

Packing the right things for a show is important for the comfort of your horse and yourself. The following checklist will help ensure that you have everything you need, and even some things that you may not end up using but should have in case of emergency.

Be sure to start by cleaning your tow vehicle and trailer thoroughly so that everything you pack stays clean and is easy to access. You should also pack the things you are least likely to need first. Put increasingly important items closer to the top where they are easy to reach. The following is a checklist of things that you should have with you if competing one horse.

Trailer items
- ☑ broom
- ☑ ties
- ☑ hay net
- ☑ spare tire
- ☑ jack

All of the checklists in this book are available by visiting our web site. Go to www.equissentials.com, click *Checklists*, and print whatever list(s) you want to use.

☑ bungee cords (for holding trunks in place while traveling or trailer escape doors open when parked)

Shipping equipment

☑ shipping bandages or boots
☑ head bumper
☑ tail bandage
☑ stable sheet, blanket, cooler
☑ 2 halters (breakable)
☑ 2 lead ropes

Barn items

☑ water buckets (2), screw eyes and double-ended hooks
☑ feed bucket (if staying overnight or if you give your horse lunch)
☑ manure fork/rake/shovel/broom
☑ manure basket or wheelbarrow
☑ bedding
☑ stall guard and screw eyes
☑ cross ties

Feed

☑ hay
☑ grain & supplements
☑ grain scoop
☑ drinking water (if your horse is reluctant to drink unfamiliar water)
☑ flavorings for water (apple cider vinegar, apple juice, peppermint, etc.)
☑ treats
☑ your horse's feed schedule

Tack

☑ saddle, girth, stirrups, and leathers
☑ foregirth, if needed
☑ saddle pad (and a spare)
☑ bridle
☑ dressage whip (not exceeding 4' in length including lash)

Rolling tack trunks, such as the one shown here, are extremely convenient for transporting equipment to competitions and work well for storage when at home. There are two saddle racks and enough room under the racks for shampoo, fly spray, coat conditioner, sponges, and other miscellaneous grooming equipment. There are wheels and handles on the back of the trunk making it easy to move around.

Extra tack hooks on either side of the trunk are handy for halters, lead ropes, spurs, and longeing equipment.

- ☑ saddle soap, sponge, and small tack cleaning bucket
- ☑ saddle rack
- ☑ tack hook
- ☑ longe line
- ☑ longe whip
- ☑ side reins
- ☑ boots or polo wraps
- ☑ mounting block

This is the top compartment of the trunk pictured on the previous page. Brushes, braiding equipment, exercise bandages, and some first aid equipment fit conveniently into this section. A less expensive alternative to tack trunks are plastic totes, which can be found at almost any department store.

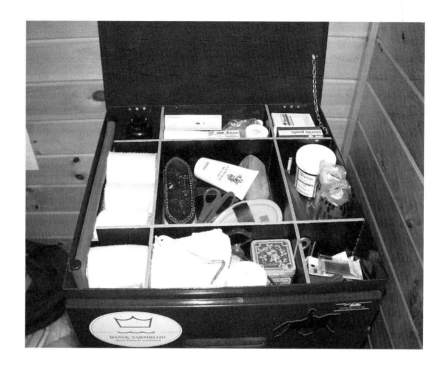

Grooming equipment

- ☑ brush box with hoof pick and a clean set of brushes (dandy brush, body brush, soft face brush, curry comb, mane comb)
- ☑ towels
- ☑ sponge
- ☑ sweat scraper
- ☑ bath bucket
- ☑ liniment
- ☑ fly spray
- ☑ coat conditioner
- ☑ tail detangler
- ☑ hoof oil or polish
- ☑ shampoo
- ☑ corn starch or baby powder (if your horse has white legs)
- ☑ scissors
- ☑ braiding kit (yarn or thread, needle, pull through, plastic clip to hold hair out of the way, water brush, white tape, mounting block)

Clothing

- ☑ breeches
- ☑ belt
- ☑ shirt – short or long-sleeved. (T-shirts and sleeveless shirts are prohibited.)
- ☑ stock tie, choker, or tie and pin
- ☑ jacket
- ☑ boots
- ☑ boot socks
- ☑ boot pull
- ☑ boot jack
- ☑ spurs (metal only)
- ☑ headgear (hunt cap, bowler, protective headgear, or top hat)
- ☑ gloves
- ☑ rain gear (clear plastic jacket and hat cover)
- ☑ mirror (side view mirror of truck works in a pinch)
- ☑ hair net
- ☑ bobby pins or rubber bands
- ☑ sunglasses
- ☑ sunblock
- ☑ street clothes
- ☑ toiletries
- ☑ bug spray
- ☑ sun hat or baseball cap

Paperwork

- ☑ Copies of the tests you will be riding
- ☑ driving directions (frequently directions are included in the Omnibus)
- ☑ truck registration
- ☑ trailer registration
- ☑ AHSA Rule Book
- ☑ Omnibus
- ☑ USDF member card
- ☑ AHSA member card
- ☑ Adult Amateur card (if you are an adult amateur)
- ☑ USDF horse registration

If driving directions are not included in the Omnibus and you have access to the Internet, go to **www.mapblast.com** and select *Drive*. After entering your starting and ending addresses, you will be provided with textual driving directions as well as maps that you can print out and carry along with you.

☑ AHSA horse registration
☑ copy of your horse's negative Coggins test
☑ copy of your horse's Rabies certificate (if required)
☑ copy of any other health certificates required by show management
☑ checkbook and wallet

Ringside items

☑ cold drink for rider
☑ water for horse
☑ towel for last minute clean up
☑ show program
☑ fly spray
☑ rider's jacket

Emergency items

☑ thermometer
☑ wound ointment
☑ Betadine or equivalent wound cleaner
☑ gauze pads
☑ scissors
☑ leg wraps and stable bandages
☑ scissors
☑ vetrap
☑ liniment
☑ alcohol
☑ clean sponges/towels
☑ phone number of vet on call

Other Indispensable Items

☑ duct tape
☑ masking tape
☑ electrical tape
☑ baling twine
☑ paper towels/tissues
☑ flashlight
☑ towelettes

- ☑ Swiss Army knife
- ☑ Aspirin or Ibuprofen
- ☑ lawn chairs
- ☑ shade tent
- ☑ water jug
- ☑ bike
- ☑ food/snacks
- ☑ carrots and other goodies
- ☑ cooler with plenty of ice and cold drinks
- ☑ extension cord
- ☑ hammer
- ☑ screwdriver
- ☑ toilet paper and/or tissues
- ☑ fan for horse's stall

Overnight Shows

In the case of shows that last for two or more days and are a long drive from your home, you will need overnight stabling as well as accommodations for yourself. Most shows offer tent stabling, and a few have permanent stabling.

The prize list will provide a listing of nearby motels and their phone numbers. Be sure to call well in advance to make reservations.

Be prepared

The prize list contains most, if not all, the information you will need to plan for an overnight show. The availability of feed, bedding, a night watchman and more, are all listed in the prize list. If the prize list does not specify the type of bedding and your horse is allergic to wood chips, for instance, be sure to bring enough bedding from home to last the duration of the show.

Although some shows do offer hay and grain, it is usually best to bring feed from home with which your horse is familiar.

Stabling

Although show management does their best to provide optimal stabling, there is much variation in the quality of tent stabling. In addition, not all

Smoking in the stabling area is strictly prohibited.

stalls are thoroughly checked when being dismantled or reassembled. Before putting your horse in a stall, carefully check to make sure that there are no nails sticking out of the walls, broken or loose boards, or any other stabling hazards. Once satisfied that the stall is safe, hang your water and feed buckets, and put fresh bedding in the stall. Install a gate or stall guard if none is provided.

Parking

You will either be given a map with your show packet that clearly indicates where trailers and trucks should be parked, or there will be signs indicating the parking areas. If the parking area is some distance from the stabling, it is usually acceptable to unload near the barn and then park your rig. Unload as quickly as possible to make room for the next person.

No Parking zones should be strictly adhered to. These zones are set up with everyone's safety in mind. In the event of a fire or other catastrophic event, fire trucks and other rescue vehicles must have easy access to the stabling area. Please keep this in mind and don't *ever* park your vehicle in a *No Parking* zone.

Consider the Other Competitors

Stabling areas at shows are typically congested, so everyone has to work to keep their equipment neatly assembled and in a small area. This makes it easier to maneuver and reduces the chances of someone getting hurt tripping over things. Although, it's undoubtedly a nuisance to be carrying bales of hay and shavings from your trailer to the stabling area, this is one of those inconveniences with which everyone has to deal.

Because the stabling area at shows is cramped, do not cross-tie your horse in a barn aisle. Use your stall for grooming, braiding, and tacking up. When bathing your horse after riding, do so well away from the stabling area so that you don't inadvertently create a swamp.

Be sure to dump manure in the areas designated by show management. This consideration on your part helps to keep the grounds neat and saves show management a lot of aggravation when cleaning up after the show.

Remember that not everyone has the same taste in music as you. If you have brought a radio or tape player to the show, keep the volume low so that it doesn't disturb other competitors.

Introduce yourself to your neighbors. If show management has not placed an emergency information card on your horse's stall door, create one for yourself and point it out to your neighbors. This card should include your name, the name and number of the hotel at which you are staying, your trainer's name and number (if she is at the show, too), and any other information that would be of use in an emergency. Make a point to see if your neighbors have an emergency contact list on their stall doors so that you will know how to reach them if needed. In addition, if there is not a night watchman, you may want to make arrangements with your neighbor(s) to take turns checking the horses.

If you had any type of electrical appliance plugged in during the day, be sure to unplug it before leaving for the evening.

When unloading equipment at the show as well as loading to leave, do not leave anything unattended. Unfortunately, equipment has been known to disappear at competitions.

Coping with Horse Show Nerves

When a number of riders were canvassed regarding their feelings about showing, they all talked about horse show nerves or fear. Not everyone was nervous about the same things, but the most common concerns included: coping with their horse's nerves, the warm-up area traffic and warming up (see the chapter entitled *Warming Up and Warm-Up Area Etiquette*), fear of forgetting the test, fear of riding in front of a judge, fear of failure, fear of elimination, and fear of looking stupid.

All of these fears are legitimate, and the good news is that all of them are manageable.

Fear

Fear, horse show nerves, stage fright, or whatever you choose to call it is a common problem. Unfortunately, fear can be detrimental to your performance as it causes you to stiffen and tighten muscles, lose your concentration, and breathe shallowly rather than deeply with your diaphragm.

It's important to learn how to cope with your fear, and there are some simple exercises that will help. Proper breathing is one of the single most important exercises. By taking deep, regular breaths, you keep oxygen flowing properly to your brain and your muscles. You will be able to think more clearly and your physical coordination will be better. As you sit reading this, take a deep breath with your mouth slightly open. Let your diaphragm expand to accommodate the deep breath. You will have a slightly bloated feeling. Exhale slowly. Practice breathing rhythmically. When you are riding at home and feel some tension, think about your breathing. Do the same thing when warming up at a show and when actually competing.

Visualizing your ride can also be helpful. As you ride your test in your mind, imagine where you will half halt in order to make smooth transitions. Visualize straight centerlines and diagonals, rhythmic gaits, and your horse moving freely forward. Think about accuracy and how you will achieve it. Be sure to imagine what you will do if your horse loses his rhythm, becomes a bit crooked, picks up the wrong canter lead and so on. By thinking about how to fix potential problems, you will be better prepared if something does go awry.

Stay focused. Although you do need to rely on your peripheral vision to avoid traffic in the warm-up area, the majority of your concentration should be on riding your horse. Think about how he feels and what you need to do (if anything) to improve the feeling. If he's a bit stiff, you might want to do some leg yielding or serpentines. If he's heavy in your hands or inattentive, transitions and changes of direction might be a good choice. The main thing is to be attentive so that you can make changes and corrections as needed.

Fear of Forgetting the Test

Start memorizing the test as far in advance as possible, and review it regularly. There are several methods for memorizing tests. You'll have to determine what works best for you. Here are some options:

1) Some people with good visualization skills and a memory for the position of the letters can memorize the test just by reading through it a number of times.
2) Another method is to make a small dressage arena in your yard or living room and walk through the test concentrating on where the transitions are and becoming familiar with the pattern.
3) You can also draw the arena on paper and make diagrams of the move-

ments to help you visualize the patterns and location of the movement in the ring.

4) If you don't mind investing some money, there are booklets available that show the different tests with diagrams of each movement. Check with your local tack shop, tack catalog, or ads in dressage magazines for more information.

Once you feel that you know the test, mentally ride it whenever possible — maybe while you're eating lunch, waiting at a long traffic light, or right before going to sleep. Use any otherwise "dead" time when you can really concentrate to practice your test. Imagine the entire test from start to finish: a nice straight entrance down the center line followed by a square, straight halt, a correct salute, and a nice transition into trot. Imagine making a smooth turn at C. Ride every step of the test in your mind thinking about where you need to make half halts so that your horse is properly prepared for each upcoming movement. Imagine riding corners and 20-meter circles with the correct amount of bend while maintaining a steady rhythm and tempo.

When riding the test, either in practice or at the show, always think two movements ahead. Do not rely on knowing just the next movement because at the end of that one, you may not be able to think of the next one quickly enough.

Finally, if you aren't confident about remembering the test, you can utilize a reader (caller).

Using a Reader (Caller)

A reader is a friend, instructor, or anyone you trust who will stand at B or E and read the test out loud to you. If you are nervous about remembering the test, a reader is a good idea. Nonetheless, you should make every effort to memorize the test so that you have some idea of where you are going just in case the reader makes a mistake. Choose someone who will read at the appropriate speed — usually one or two movements ahead of where you are — and with a clear voice that will carry the length of the arena. Be sure to explain to your reader that she must read the test *exactly* as it is written. To do otherwise could be considered outside assistance, which is illegal and can lead to elimination.

Readers are not permitted in championship, FEI level, or Freestyle classes.

Because warming up is a very important element to competing, an entire chapter entitled "Warming Up and Warm-Up Area Etiquette" is devoted to this topic.

If the reader thinks that you have not heard her, she can repeat herself. However, if you should make a mistake, the reader cannot repeat the instructions. The judge will ring the bell (or blow the whistle) and tell you where your mistake was. Once you are back on course, your reader may resume reading the test.

Having a competent reader may help to minimize the chance of your going off course and can do much to soothe frayed nerves.

Coping with Your Horse's Show Nerves

People and horses both tend to get a little nervous in unfamiliar settings. There are a number of things that you can do to help your horse and yourself acclimate to a new environment before the actual show day. You can take your horse to an unfamiliar place before the show and work him there. Ideally, you could trailer him to your instructor's farm so that you have the advantage of your instructor's assistance as you introduce him to a new setting. The next best thing would be to go to a friend's house and ride your horse there, with the friend standing by to help out if needed.

You can also contact local barns and inquire if you can school in their ring. Most farms will require that you sign a release form, pay a fee to cover insurance, and bring a current copy of your Coggins test or other health certificates with you.

If you can't work your horse at another location before the show, you aren't out of luck. Plan to get to the show two or more hours earlier than necessary. When you arrive, get your horse out of the trailer, remove his leg wraps, and hand walk him around the show grounds. Let him see all the sights and have a chance to become accustomed to his new environment. When he settles, you can either find a quiet place to longe him, or you can warm him up under saddle. After working him, cool him out, and return him to your trailer or stall (if you have one). Offer him water and let him relax and munch on hay.

Based on his behavior during your initial warmup, you can make an educated guess as to the amount of time you will need for the final warmup before your test. You can also take him for additional walks in hand around the grounds. If it's a hot day and your horse was very quiet and obedient, a final 10-minute warmup before your test will probably be sufficient. On the other hand, if he is still fresh and it's a brisk day, you may want to plan for a longer warmup.

Fear of Riding in Front of a Judge and Spectators

Most people agree that getting over the fear of riding in front of a judge and spectators comes with time and experience. The more you do it, the easier it becomes. In time, you become more comfortable in new settings, and so does your horse. You realize that the judge is not your adversary, but someone who is trying to help you with your training by objectively evaluating where you are at at a particular point in time. As you gain more experience competing, you will become more ring savvy. You will learn how to gain valuable points by being more precise and more fluid and by being able to showcase your horse's strong points while finessing his weak areas.

Even at your first show, you will probably be surprised at how quickly you forget the judge, spectators, and any other distractions as soon as you're heading down the centerline.

Fear of Failure

Most everyone is afraid of failure, but failure is a subjective term and unproductive to dwell on. Competitors (in any discipline) need to concentrate on what they learn from a competition rather than agonizing over the results on the scoreboard. Every show can be beneficial and educational if you view it as such. There is no such thing as "failure" if you can finish the day with some newly acquired knowledge or skill. Learning something new is a reward in itself, no matter the score or the ribbon.

You have worked long and hard to get to a competition where you can show off your horse of whom you are undoubtedly and justifiably proud. Enjoy the day regardless of the results and try to get a friend to go along who can take some pictures.

Fear of Elimination

Fear of Elimination is certainly valid. The rules in the AHSA Rulebook clearly state what infractions result in elimination. Most of the rules are quite straightforward and don't leave much room for speculation. Refer to *Appendix C*

For a more complete list of rules surrounding elimination, see *Appendix C.*

for more detailed information on infractions that can lead to elimination.

It is important to reread the rules at least once a year. Be sure to read any emergency rule changes in the AHSA's quarterly magazine, *Horse Show*. In addition to the AHSA rules, always read rules for specific competitions (e.g. some competitions don't allow dogs, others don't allow campers, etc.). Don't allow yourself to be eliminated for completely preventable reasons.

Three of the most common grounds for elimination are:

• Being late for your test.
• Your horse jumping out of the arena (all four feet).
• Four errors (being off course).

To avoid being eliminated by being late for your test, be sure that your watch is set to the official show time and keep track of the rider before you. Remember that once the judge rings the bell for you to begin, you have one minute in which to enter the arena. At competitions where several arena are set side by side, it can be difficult to know if the starting bell or whistle was sounded for you or the rider in the ring next to yours. When in doubt, it's all right to ask the judge. However, once you begin the test, you may not speak with anyone.

The second cause for elimination as listed above is usually preventable. Occasionally a very young horse is spooked so badly that he will jump out of the arena, but it's rare. What isn't so rare is when the rider doesn't pay careful enough attention while passing **A**, and the horse leaves through the open gate. Officials are NOT required to close the gate, so be particularly conscientious when riding the **A** side of the arena.

Going off course is a case of not having memorized your test sufficiently, being overwhelmed by show nerves, or having an inexperienced reader. With more practice, this won't be an obstacle.

In cases of elimination due to four errors of course or the horse leaving the arena with all four feet, most judges will encourage the competitor to finish the test if time permits. If this should happen to you, take advantage of this opportunity if it's offered to you. This is excellent experience for you and your horse — completing the test is an important accomplishment as well as being a confidence builder.

Other grounds for elimination are use of drugs, professionals riding in classes designated Amateur only, use of illegal equipment, etc.

Fear of Looking Stupid

It takes a lot of hard work, courage, dedication, determination, and stamina to compete. You should be proud of yourself for having the mettle to get yourself and your horse to a show. Experienced competitors understand and sympathize with what newcomers are going through, and most spectators would like to be in your boots.

Even people who have been competing for years have their embarrassing moments. I once witnessed a situation in which a Grand Prix rider, whose student had put her double bridle together with the curb and snaffle reins reversed, didn't notice until a judge commented on it…at the end of her test!

Don't ever forget that the reason you decided to do this was to have fun. If it stops being fun, you need to evaluate why and make the necessary changes. Maybe you are trying to do too much single-handedly, maybe your horse would be better off doing a few more shows at one level lower than you are at, or maybe you need to find more reliable transportation. When problems arise, make a prioritized list according to which problems are easy to fix and which may require more effort or expense. Then, go about remedying them so that you can get back to the business of having fun.

Practicing the Test

There are varying opinions regarding whether or not you should practice your test at home. Some people believe that too much practice will cause the horse to start anticipating and performing movements before being asked. It is true that constant repetition of a particular test could lead to this.

On the other hand, if you never ride the test all the way through from start to finish, you won't know for sure which parts of the test are more challenging to you and your horse than others. It's important to ride through the test in its entirety at least once in a while so that you can identify your weak areas and work on them. Once you have figured that out, ride bits and pieces of the test — but in the wrong order to avoid having your horse anticipate the movements. Pay particular attention to the movements that you find more difficult.

Day of the Show

On show day, your horse is going to be relying on you to lead the way. This is why it's important to be sensitive to his needs and to make sure that he is comfortable. This is also why you want to be well prepared so that your nerves don't get the better of you, which will undoubtedly be a factor in how he handles his new surroundings.

Stay focused on getting him to relax and to perform as closely as possible to the way he performs at home. There is more traffic, and you are in unfamiliar settings, but if you lead by making no big deal of it, he's much more likely to follow. If he's upset, don't become angry with him. There's a lot going on and he needs time to acclimate.

View the show as part of the process and not just an end result. You will be able to relax and learn more, in this relaxed state of mind.

Suggested Reading

Gahwyler, Max   *The Competitive Edge*
Savoie, Jane   *That Winning Feeling*

Warming Up & Warm-Up Area Etiquette

A correct warm-up can mean the difference between a smooth, polished performance and a not so successful performance. It is a skill that you will develop over time with each particular horse you compete.

Determining the Length of Your Warm-Up

Unless you have firsthand information from someone who has competed your horse, there is no way of knowing for sure what your ideal warm-up time and method should be. At first, the best you can do is to make an educated guess.

Warm-up length is dependent on several factors: your horse's show experience (or lack thereof), your show experience (or lack thereof), the weather, your horse's temperament, and the level of activity in the warm-up area. For example, if you have a fit, nervous horse, the show grounds are very hectic, and it's a cool breezy day, you will probably need a longer warm-up than someone with a very quiet horse on a warm day at a sparsely attended show.

Although longeing can be a good method of warming up a horse, it should not be done in a show setting unless you are sure you can maintain control. A loose horse is a danger to himself as well as other horses and riders.

If your horse is excitable, or you think that he may be, you will probably want to hand walk him around the premises to accustom him to the level of activity and the different sights. You may even choose to longe him if there is an appropriate longeing area. Since longeing can be disruptive to other horses and riders, check with the show manager to see if there is an area specifically designated for longeing. If not, stay in a corner of the general warm up area well out of the way of riders. It is inadvisable for two people to longe in the same warm up area. Either wait until the other person is through longeing, or find a different area.

For a horse new to the show environment, it's a good idea to arrive at the show early enough to introduce him to all the sights and work him under saddle until he's feeling relaxed and focused. He can then go back to his stall or trailer until his final warm-up 10 to 15 minutes before your actual test.

The opposite of the above scenario is the lazy horse on a hot, humid day in a not-very-busy warm-up area. This is the type of horse who would probably do well with only 10 to 20 minutes of warm up. Determining the right length and type of warm up is a skill that is developed over time.

Warm-Up Areas

The show management will make it known where you can warm up. You will either be provided with a map of the show grounds with the arenas and warm-up areas clearly marked, or there will be cordoned off areas that are not available for warming up. Prize lists sometimes specify the footing in the arenas as well as the warm-up areas.

With very few exceptions, the competition arenas are not to be used for warming up. Occasionally, when an indoor arena is being used as a competition arena and there is not a suitable warmup area outside the arena, riders are permitted to warm-up in the arena for a minute or two before their test commences. The ring steward will let you know if this is acceptable.

Warm-Up Area Etiquette

Warm-up area etiquette is about safety and consideration for everyone involved. Certain guidelines combined with common sense and courtesy should be adhered to. The following are some basic guidelines, rather than rules, that will help you while warming up.

- It's generally accepted that you pass other riders left shoulder to left shoulder.
- Slower (walk) traffic should stay to the inside.
- Keep at least one horse's length away from any other horse.
- Give riders who are on circles or performing more advanced movements the right of way.
- Do not cut in front of other riders.
- When overtaking traffic in the same direction, pass on the inside with care and plenty of clearance. Otherwise, make a circle or cut across the ring to avoid passing.
- Be careful how you use your whip and voice so that you don't accidentally cause another rider's horse to react.
- Give green horses and/or riders extra room.
- When walking, practicing halts, or riding pirouettes, stay to the inside.
- Do not halt on the track as riders behind you have no way of knowing your intentions.
- If another horse becomes unruly and/or deposits its rider, walk to the middle and halt until the situation is under control. If the horse gets loose, announce to other riders "Loose horse!" so that they are not caught by surprise.
- Stay at least 15 meters away from the competition arena when in use.
- If you are going to longe your horse, do so in a corner or an area where you won't be in other people's way.

Always keep in mind that there may be someone who doesn't know the rules of passing, or who may be on a green or unruly horse. Make allowances as needed. Someday *you* may be riding that green, unruly horse.

Don't be shy about calling out to another rider to make your intentions known. Unless you know the other rider, don't assume that they know where they should be in relation to you. Whether you are passing another rider head on or from behind, be sure to call out "inside" or "outside" well in advance to avoid a collision.

Be willing to yield to a rider who is having a problem or is schooling a movement (e.g. a half pass), and be sure to thank riders who afford you this same courtesy.

When unsure about warm-up area etiquette, let courtesy and safety prevail.

To reduce traffic, leave the warm-up area when through warming up.

Warm-Up Area Equipment

Be sure to place your horse's number(s) on his bridle whenever you are working him, whether you are longeing him, riding him in the warm-up area, or competing. Failure to do so can result in elimination. If you should lose your number, contact the show manager or secretary immediately.

Equipment that is strictly forbidden in the competition arena but may be used in the warm-up area includes:

- Running martingales (with snaffle bridle only).
- Single direct side reins but only when longeing the horse. It is illegal to ride a horse in side reins.
- Exercise boots (including "easy boots").
- Leg or tail bandages.
- Nose covers.
- Standard longeing whip.
- Two whips no longer than 6' including the lash.
- Horses at Fourth level and above may warm up in a snaffle bridle.

The Coach's Role and Fees

If your coach is at the show with you, he can warm up your horse for you provided you are not competing in a championship competition. Championship competitions specifically state that only the competitor may warm up the horse. A groom can ride the horse from the stabling area to the arena, for instance, so long as he does so on a long rein at the walk.

Check with your trainer ahead of time to see what coaching services he offers and how much he charges. Some coaches will help their students warm up as well as watch and evaluate the actual test if time permits. This can be a very valuable service, but it can also be expensive. Arrangements for coaching should be made at least several days before the show.

Bit and Whip Checks

At recognized competitions, it is not uncommon for the ring steward, at the direction of the technical delegate, to check whips and bits at the conclusion of your test. The ring steward can randomly select any rider for an

Rule infractions that occur in the competition ring are the domain of the judge. Infractions that occur outside of the competition ring are the responsibility of the technical delegate. However, if a judge notices an illegal activity or use of illegal equipment outside of the competition arena, she may draw the TD's attention to it.

equipment check. Her role is to make sure that riders are conforming to tack and attire rules as set forth by the AHSA. The use of an illegal bit can result in elimination. In cases where bit inspections require contact with the inside of the horse's mouth, the ring steward must wear a clean protective glove for each horse and/or disinfect their hands after each inspection.

Whips in excess of 4' including the lash are illegal. If your whip is a few inches more than 4' including the lash, you can usually bring it to 4' or less by removing the lash.

Remember that the horse, rider, or handler must be wearing the number whenever the horse is being ridden or exercised.

Saluting

All dressage tests begin with the rider entering at A, halting at X, and saluting the judge — with two notable exceptions: there is no halt at the beginning of either of the Introductory level tests, and riders performing freestyles may halt and salute wherever they like.

The salute is a sign of respect for the judge and tells the judge that you are ready to begin your test. After you have saluted, the judge will acknowledge you with a nod of the head or some other gesture that will indicate to you that you may begin the test. Do not proceed, especially at the beginning of the test, until the judge acknowledges your salute. The judge will acknowledge you by nodding her head or sitting down if she has been standing. If you do proceed without her acknowledgement, she can ring the bell and mark it as an error.

At the end of the test, you will again halt and salute the judge. She will acknowledge your final salute, and you may proceed out of the arena at a walk on a long rein.

The salute begins with a good halt. Although this halt is not absolutely square, Daktara is straight, immobile, and well balanced over all four legs. Susan's position is exemplary.

Susan demonstrates the correct method for saluting when carrying the whip in the right hand; she wraps the fingers of her left hand around the whip handle so that she can salute with her right hand.

Daktara's face has dropped slightly behind the vertical so that her poll is no longer the highest point as it should be. (Note the square saddle pad that protects the tail of Susan's shadbelly coat from dirt and sweat).

Making a Good First Impression

First impressions as well as last impressions count for a great deal. This is why it is paramount that you make a nice, straight entrance on the centerline, followed by a smooth, straight halt. The halt is described as being attentive, motionless, and straight. A well-executed halt demonstrates your mastery of the aids for halt and your horse's obedience. The halt is not a movement that you should wait to practice until the day before the show. It should be a part of your daily schooling. Your attention to this will serve you well not only from the standpoint of your horse's obedience, but also from the standpoint of being able to execute a good halt in a competition setting.

You should also be practicing your salutes on a regular basis. If you wait until the last minute, you could discover at the show that it's not as easy as you had thought to keep your horse in the halt with only one hand on the reins. It also takes some practice to handle the reins and whip gracefully with the left hand as you salute with the right. You will want to feel confident that you are saluting correctly, and this type of confidence is achieved only through sufficient practice at home.

The final turn down the centerline must also be straight, and your final halt should be attentive, motionless, and straight followed by a proper salute as described below. This is your last chance to make an impression on the judge. Be sure that you don't get sloppy towards the end of the test even though you and your horse may be tired.

Saluting: The Female Competitor

Although the AHSA rules state that "riders take the reins in one hand" and don't specify which hand, it is customary to salute with the right hand. When your horse is standing quietly, take the reins in your left hand, incline your head in a slight bow, and let your right arm drop loosely to your side. Make your salute graceful and prompt but not hurried. As you lift your head, pick up the right rein with your right hand. As soon as the judge acknowledges you, proceed with your test, or exit the arena if you have finished.

Saluting: The Male Competitor

A man may salute as described above, or he may choose to remove his hat with the hand that he uses to salute. Avoid showing the interior of the hat to

Even if there are judges seated at B and E, you should only salute the judge seated at C.

the judge while saluting. Only riders in uniform may use the military salute. Men wearing helmets with safety harnesses should not remove their helmet.

What Everyone Needs to Know About Saluting

Look directly at the judge as you salute. Lower your hand and then nod your head straight forward and down in a quick motion. Your nod should be brief so that you don't risk missing the judge's acknowledgement of your salute. While nodding, remain tall and elegant in the saddle and don't round your shoulders. A correct position will serve you well as you make your transition from the halt to whatever gait is called for next.

When saluting, do not drop the hand that is carrying the whip. If you are carrying a whip in your right hand and intend to salute with that hand, grasp the whip with the fingers of your left hand before saluting. You do not need to switch the whip to the left side as it could prove awkward.

The Final Halt is Not Always at X

Although the first halt is always at X (with the exceptions noted earlier), this is not the case with the final salute. Be sure to read your test(s) carefully as the final halt is sometimes at G.

It is the rider's responsibility to keep careful track of the time and be at the in gate when it's her turn to compete. Ruth has set her watch to the official show time and checks to see how much time she has left for warming up. Photo: Mary Phelps

Riding the Test

Although the intention of this book is to provide readers with information on the rules and protocols surrounding dressage competitions, it would seem remiss not to include some basics on actual test riding.

Before Entering at A

If you are fortunate enough to have a friend or family member grooming for you, ask that person to be ready at the in-gate with a clean cloth to give your horse and your boots a last minute wipe. That person can also make sure that your horse's tail is still looking neat and tidy, remove exercise boots or bandages that you may have been using while warming up, and make sure that your horse's number is firmly attached to his bridle. If the show at which you are competing does not have a ring steward, your helper(s) can keep track of and advise you on the horse that competes just before you so that you have some idea as to how much time you have left to warm up.

This is a good time to offer your horse a drink of water and to have one yourself.

The Final Warm-up

Your final warm-up before the test significantly impacts your horse's performance in the ring. A good warm-up gets you both off on the right foot. Once the rider ahead of you makes his final salute and the ring steward indicates it's alright, you can start riding your horse around the outside of the arena. Now is the perfect time to show your horse the judge's box and anything else that he may find scary. Time permitting, it is wise to ride past the judge's box in both directions. During this final warm-up, you can practice whatever you need to, or whatever your coach (if you have one) recommends. You can work on transitions, small circles, shallow loops, or whatever you think best suits your horse's needs at the moment.

The way your horse feels as you warm-up around the outside of the ring will help you determine what to work on during those final moments before your test. If he is heavy in your hands, you may choose to practice transitions to get him softer and listening. If he's feeling a bit lazy, you could also do transitions to sharpen him up, or you could do some medium and extended work depending on his level of training. The important thing is that you identify what doesn't feel quite up to par and use this time to address it. Your efforts will be rewarded by your horse's responsiveness to you during the test.

Calm, Forward and Straight

Stay focused on remaining calm, keeping your horse relaxed, riding forward, and riding your horse as though nothing is different.

As discussed in the chapter entitled *Deciding What Level to Enter*, you should be confident that you and your horse can proficiently perform everything that is asked for in a particular test. This will help your confidence level, which directly influences your horse's confidence. Your horse is going to be relying on you to lead the way. This is why proper preparation is so important — so that your nerves don't hinder your performance and adversely affect your horse's reaction to his new surroundings.

The Whistle, the Bell, and Other Sounding Devices

The judge will use a bell, whistle or other sounding device to let you know

This is 4 year old Nebraska's first show, so Candi wisely chooses to show him the judge's booth. She walks him past in one direction, and turns and walks him back so that he has the opportunity to see it from both directions. It's not uncommon for green horses to find the judge's booth scary.

Moments later Candi and Nebraska trot confidently down the centerline straight toward the judge's booth. Time spent showing Nebraska the booth was time well spent.

Although Nebraska displays an energetic, ground covering trot, he is slightly on his forehand with his face a bit behind the vertical — not uncommon mistakes for such a young horse. As you can see, Candi is actively driving him forward with her legs to correct this problem.

The One-Minute Rule — Once the judge has signaled with the bell, whistle, or other sounding device that you may begin your test, you have one minute in which to enter the ring. Failure to do so will result in elimination.

that she is ready for you to begin your test. Once the bell has been rung, you have one minute in which to enter the arena. Failure to do so can result in elimination.

When multiple arenas are set-by side, show managers will put signs next to the arenas to indicate their number. The manager will also usually write the type of sounding device being used below the ring number. This is particularly useful at some of the larger shows where three or four side-by-side arenas can make it very difficult to tell which judge is signaling whom.

The judge can use the whistle or bell any time during your ride to indicate that you are off course, that your horse is lame, or that you have broken a rule (e.g. you are carrying a whip in a championship class, your horse is wearing boots, your whip is too long, etc.). When the judge blows the whistle, stop to find out the problem.

Should you go off course, stop and let the judge redirect you.

In the case of errors (such as going off course), there is a two-point penalty for the first error, four points for the second, eight points for the third, and elimination for the fourth.

Making an Entrance

Your test begins when you enter at A and is finished after your final salute. When the judge rings the bell, you have one minute in which to enter the ring. If your horse feels good, go straight in. Otherwise, use this time to your advantage. Even if the judge has rung the bell and you are headed towards A, you can still make a last-minute circle if needed. As soon as you head down the centerline, your job is to show off your horse's strong points and finesse his weak points.

As you enter at A, focus on C so that you remain straight on the centerline. You will have to decide how far in advance of X to half halt in order to produce a smooth halt at X. It is better to err on the side of performing a good halt that is a little too early or late. The judge would rather see a smooth, flowing halt that's slightly off of X, than one that is exactly at X but abrupt, hollow, crooked, unbalanced, or a combination of these things.

Once your horse is immobile in the halt, salute the judge. When the judge acknowledges you, move away smoothly and promptly — with smooth being your priority. Again, head straight toward **C** and make a smooth turn, keeping your horse moving energetically forward. The turns at **C** are very tight (10-meters), so you will need to help your horse through them by keeping him active and energetic but not quick. It's not unusual for a horse new to the competition scene to be reluctant to trot boldly towards the judge's booth.

Remember to ride your horse thoughtfully and purposefully, and concentrate on the quality of his gaits rather than fixating on riding from one letter to the next. This is easier said than done and comes primarily with experience.

Circles

It's not uncommon to see novices ride into the corners when performing 20-meter circles at A or C. When circles start at A or C, the corner before A or C is ridden as a corner, but the very next corner is part of the circle. Ride it as such.

It's easy to determine where the 20-meter circles are in the small arena (20-meters x 40-meters). They are the full width of the arena and exactly half the length. Ideally, you will be able to practice ahead of time in an arena that is the same size as the one in which you will be competing.

Circles of 15-meters are 2/3 the width of the arena, and 10-meter circles are exactly half the arena width.

The circle shape is extremely important — not just because of its bearing on your score but because of its training value. Circles are the corner stone of a horse's training. If your horse is not performing a round circle, he is not correctly balanced or on the aids. Circles improve a horse's balance, suppleness, engagement, and obedience to your aids. Be sure to maintain an even bend throughout the circle.

Corners

How deeply you ride into the corners depends upon your horse's training and the level at which you are competing. The higher the level, the deeper you should ride the corner, but never to the detriment of the overall performance. At training level, corners will be considerably more shallow than

See Appendix E for detailed drawings of various sized circles originating at different points in the arena.

those performed by a Grand Prix horse because a training level horse does not yet have the strength, balance, or suppleness to go deeply into a corner.

Transitions

Smooth transitions should be one of your priorities. They demonstrate that you are keeping your horse obediently on the aids. Additionally, a good transition ensures that at least the first few strides of the next gait will be good. A bad transition ensures the exact opposite. It's difficult to recover from a poor transition, which is why so much emphasis is placed on them. At first, be satisfied with a smooth transition even if it is not exactly at the letter. This shows good riding and training on your part. As you and your horse become more proficient, it will be easy to perform good transitions at the marker.

The Gaits

The quality of your horse's gaits should be uppermost in your mind. Relaxation of the horse's back is a specific judging criterion that appears in the Collective Marks section of all AHSA tests. Remember that the Collective Marks in all AHSA tests have coefficients of two to emphasize their importance.

Rhythm and tempo are very important in a horse's training as described in the chapter, *The Purpose of the Movements*. Rhythm is the number of beats in a gait; walk is a four-beat gait, trot is a two-beat gait, and canter is a three-beat gait. Ideally, the rhythm should remain regular and pure. Tempo is the speed of the gait — the number of times the horse's feet hit the ground in a given period of time. Maintaining a correct rhythm and tempo will help you in all of your work.

The Walk

The walk rhythm is four beats. The four types of walk called for in competition include collected, medium, extended, and free walk. In the past, Training level called for working walk, but this has since been changed to medium. The walk is too frequently passed over when training, hence the emphasis now being placed on it in tests and in the frequent coefficients of two for walk work. Test designers realize the importance of the walk, and they

There should be four distinct beats in the walk, and the horse should show a clear "V" with the inside hind and inside front leg and then the outside hind and outside front. This picture was taken a split second before the moment where a clear "V" would be visible. Nonetheless, you can see that it will happen. Notice the nice soft connection that Susan has with Daktara's mouth and the straight line from the bit to Susan's hand to her elbow. You can also draw a straight line from Susan's ear, through her elbow, her hip, and heel. This is ideal.

emphasize it by the directives and through use of coefficients. They expect competitors to heed this information and use it to improve their horses.

Some horses are born with walks that are less than ideal. Other horses may have normal walks that are accidentally corrupted through poor riding and training. The walk should always be a clear four beats, with each leg moving independently. The lateral walk, or pace, is severely penalized. This is a walk in which the horse moves his legs forward in lateral pairs, hence the term "lateral walk." When viewing a horse from the side, you should see the inside front and hind legs form a "V" shape for a brief moment, and then the outside front and hind forming a "V."

The Trot

The trot is a two-beat gait of which there are four types: collected, working, medium, and extended. Because the trot is a two-beat gait, it is the easiest gait to improve. It's easy to count the beats, feel when the rhythm has been lost, and to make corrections as needed.

Collected trot — Susan
and Daktara

Medium trot — Notice the
increased length of stride as
well as the lengthening of
Daktara's neck.

The Canter

The canter is a three-beat gait, of which there are four types: collected, working, medium, and extended.

Purity of gait is important in every gait. A common mistake in the canter is the four-beat rather than the true three-beat canter. A four-beat canter is incorrect and will lead to difficulties further down the road when you work on canter half passes, flying changes, pirouettes, etc. Judges heavily penalize the four-beat canter.

It's relatively easy to count out the beat of the canter in your head while riding: 1-2-3 1-2-3 1-2-3 and so on. The beats should be clear and evenly spaced. If not, the horse is not properly engaged. Incorrect training and a stiff back are just two possible explanations for a four-beat canter. With your trainer's help, you will be able to determine the cause of your horse's incorrect canter, and use the appropriate exercises to fix it.

When Mistakes Happen

Mistakes do happen — even to the best and most experienced competitors. Your task is to minimize the damage and focus on the next movement. Once a mistake has occurred, absolutely nothing is gained by spending another instant thinking about it. In fact, focusing on the mistake will interfere with your next movement or movements.

As an old aviation saying goes, "The runway behind you is of no use." Fortunately, it's not such a potentially life-or-death situation when it comes to riding, but it's exactly the same premise. You can't do anything about what's behind you, but you still have the ability to influence upcoming events.

If you take the time to watch experienced competitors — particularly those riding green horses — you will be impressed by how quickly they can recover from a serious mistake or disobedience and still have a nice test with a respectable score. You can do the same by keeping your emotions out of the show ring and dealing with the issues at hand. I once saw a rider go off course three times and still win the test because of the overall excellence of her ride. The rider remained focused on riding the horse rather than panicking over and dwelling on her mistakes.

It is against the rules to approach a judge to discuss your test. You may only speak with a judge about your ride if you have received permission from the technical delegate.

If you must scratch from a test for any reason, be sure to advise show management of your scratch. Failing to show up for your ride is not acceptable.

From the time the judge rings the bell indicating that you can start your test to the time that you exit the arena, you may not speak to your reader or any friends. Be sure that your friends understand that they should not speak to you either.

Exiting the Arena

Your horse and you are understandably tired. But the test is not over until after the final salute. Don't "coast" along for the last one or two movements, as you will sacrifice points needlessly. Be sure that you make a nice clean turn onto the centerline, head straight for the judge, and perform a straight, smooth halt. After the final halt and salute, you can ride one horse's length forward, turn in either direction, and exit the arena. You are not required to ride all the way to C. Do NOT circle at A before exiting.

No matter what *you* might think of your ride, keep an upbeat expression and smile if you can! Tests almost always look better than we think because we tend to be our own harshest critics.

At schooling shows, judges will occasionally (when they have the time) stop you after your ride to offer some helpful suggestions. Important information can be garnered from these short conversations — take note of what they tell you and be sure to thank them for their time and input. Do not start up a conversation with the judge asking for a blow-by-blow rundown of the test or for training tips. Accept what is offered and be on your way.

General Tips

Should anything untoward occur during your test so that you wish to be excused, you must ask for and receive the judge's permission before exiting. Failure to do so will cause the Show Committee to disqualify you from that class as well as any other classes you are entered in at this competition. All prizes and entry fees for the competition will be forfeited.

- Using your voice in any way during the test — talking to your horse, clucking, or any other sound — is against the rules. Each occurrence is treated as an error.
- If you are performing a rising trot across the diagonal followed by a sitting trot in the corner, there is no need to change diagonals. If you are to continue on in rising trot, you can change the diagonal as you cross X or when you get to the corner marker. The choice is yours. Do whatever will make for a smoother performance.
- If your horse gets behind your leg (is not attentive to your aids), don't be afraid to tap him with the whip. Letting him slouch around will adversely affect your entire ride, but tactful use of the whip may very well improve your horse's performance.
- Some riders become timid riding a test and ride too conservatively. Don't be afraid to make a mistake. It's better to do some experimenting to see what your horse needs than to be "frozen" in the saddle. Ride your horse with the same resolve with which you would ride him at home.

- Once you have a few shows behind you, dare to be bold and take some chances. Take some risks, and go for that little bit more than in your last test.
- You may ride more than one level at a show, but they must be contiguous levels. For instance, you can ride Training and First level, First and Second level, Second and Third, and so on. But you may not ride First and Third, Second and Fourth, etc.

Susan and Daktara performing a shoulder-in. The shoulder-in is an excellent collecting and bending exercise. It first appears at Second level. Photo: Mary Phelps

- Once a recognized competition commences, you may not withdraw or remove your horse(s) from the show grounds without permission from the show secretary.
- View the show as part of the process and not just as an end result. You will be able to relax more and learn more in this relaxed state of mind.

Directives, Collective Marks, and Coefficients

It is essential that you be aware of the Directives, Collective Marks, and Coefficients. Not just because of how they affect your score, but because of their importance in your horse's training.

If you look at a test sheet, you will see the movement that you are to perform in the left column, under the heading "Test." The "Directive Ideas," in the next column to the right, explain to the judge and competitor alike what is being stressed in each particular movement. For example, a test movement might be *HXF Lengthen stride in trot rising, F Working trot sitting*, with the directive idea being *Straightness, quality of trots and transitions.*

Collective Marks are the marks at the bottom of the test. They include:

* *Gaits* — freedom and regularity
* *Impulsion* — desire to move forward, elasticity of the steps, relaxation of the back
* *Submission* — attention and confidence; harmony, lightness and ease of movements; acceptance of the bit
* Rider's position and seat; correctness and effect of the aids

With the exception of Introductory level, all Collective Marks carry a coefficient of two.

Suggested Reading

Gen. Jonathon S. Burton, *How to Ride a Winning Dressage Test*
Dr. Max Gahwyler, *The Competitive Edge*

Scoring

Scoring serves several purposes, with the most obvious being the ranking of riders in a particular test. But it also serves two other important purposes: it tells you where you are at a particular moment in time, and it provides you with information that may be of value to you in your training. For the numbers to be useful, you must understand their meaning.

The Range of Scores

Scores are assigned for each movement in a test. They range from 0 indicating that the movement was not performed to 10, which is excellent. 10 is a score that is not frequently seen, and 0 is a score none of us *ever* wants to see. The AHSA definition of the scores is as follows:

10	Excellent
9	Very good
8	Good
7	Fairly good
6	Satisfactory
5	Sufficient
4	Insufficient

3	Fairly bad
2	Bad
1	Very bad
0	Not executed

Coefficients

Scoring is relatively straightforward, but scorers must not forget to take into account coefficients. Some movements within the test carry a coefficient of 2 while all of the collective marks in AHSA tests — the marks that appear at the bottom of the score sheet — have coefficients of 2. When you ride a movement that has a coefficient of 2, the score is multiplied by 2. In other words, a score of 6 now becomes 12.

Always study your tests carefully to ascertain which movements carry coefficients. For instance, at First level Test 1 (1999) the trot serpentine, free walk on the diagonal, and the 20-meter circle in which the horse is asked to stretch down, all have coefficients of 2. The serpentine demonstrates the horse's suppleness and willingness to change from one bend to another; the free walk on the diagonal is important because it shows the purity of the horse's walk; and the stretching down trot circle shows his willingness to stretch into the bridle without falling on his forehand.

Coefficients are used to acknowledge the difficulty of a movement and to underscore its significance in the horse's training. The free walk is a good example. In a number of the tests, a coefficient is assigned to the free walk because of its importance in a horse's training. As you read through the tests, pay special attention to the coefficient movements.

Collective Marks

At the bottom of the test sheet are the Collective Marks, all of which carry coefficients of 2 (with the exception of Introductory level). Collective Marks are the scores assigned by the judge in four distinct areas. These areas include:

- *Gaits* — (freedom and regularity)
- *Impulsion* — (desire to move forward, elasticity of the steps, suppleness of the back, engagement of the hindquarters)
- *Submission* — (attention and confidence; harmony, lightness and ease

of movements, acceptance of the bridle)

• Rider's position and seat; correctness and effect of the aids

The Process of Scoring

Each test has a certain number of movements in it and a maximum number of points that can be earned. The judge assigns a score from 0 to 10 for each movement.

To arrive at the final score, the scorer adds up the scores for each individual movement — being careful to take coefficients into account. From this total, the scorer deducts penalty points if there were any. The total score is then divided by the total number of points possible to arrive at a score that is expressed as a percentage. For example, a maximum of 220 points can be earned in Training level Test 1 (1999). Therefore, if a rider earns a total of 150 points in Training level test 1, the score of 150 points is divided by 220. The final score is 68.181%. Scores are typically carried out to three decimal places.

Breaking Ties

When two competitors earn the same total score, the competitor with the highest marks in the *Collective Marks* section will be declared the winner. For example, let's assume that two competitors are tied for first place in Training level Test 1 with a total score of 145 points (or 65.909%). Competitor One scored 99 points for the test and 46 points for the *Collective Marks*. Competitor Two, on the other hand, scored 97 points for the test but 48 points for the *Collective Marks*. In this example, Competitor Two will be declared the winner because she scored higher in the *Collective Marks* section.

However, if both competitors have identical scores for the test and the *Collective Marks*, the judge can do one of two things: not break the tie, or review the tests in order to determine the winner. It's not unusual for a judge to remember something exceptional from one of the tests that helps her make a decision. For example, one horse might have had smoother transitions; or they both may have been quite equal, but one horse occasionally ground his teeth or swished his tail, in which case the horse that didn't display any resistances to his rider would receive the higher placing.

When there are more than 25 entries in a class, the class must be divided. Exceptions to this are AHSA/USDF Championships and USET Championships, qualifying and selection trials, and observation classes.

In the case of a tie where prize money is involved, the money is divided evenly, but the judge may have to break the tie to facilitate the awarding of ribbons and trophies.

Save Your Tests

It's valuable to save your tests for several reasons. Much can be learned by comparing tests over the course of a show season. If you aren't fortunate enough to have regular instruction, these test sheets can help point you in the right direction. For instance, if you are repeatedly receiving 8's from different judges for your 20-meter trot circles, then you can be secure in the knowledge that the quality of the trot, your horse's bend on the circle, and the size and shape of the circle are good. On the other hand, if you are consistently receiving 4's for your halts from several different judges, and they are all commenting that your halts are not straight, then you obviously need to address this problem. Test sheets can serve as a road map in your training by highlighting your strengths as well as your weaknesses.

If you are pursuing USDF year end awards, it's imperative that you save your test sheets so that you can check your records with the USDF's before the end of the competition year. If there are any mistakes in the recording of scores, it is your responsibility to bring them to the attention of the USDF.

Considering the Scores

There is no denying that scoring is subjective. Although judges for recognized competitions must be certified for the level they are judging and go through rigorous training programs in order to get this certification, they are still human beings with their own preferences. Furthermore, some judges are more generous than others. One judge may watch a nice, fluid test with some small inaccuracies and give it a high score while another judge, who may focus more on precision, will not be so generous with this same competitor. This is why the comments are of such value to you in understanding your performance, and in helping you determine what you need to concentrate on in your training.

It's important to be aware of the vicissitudes of judging when reviewing your tests. For instance, if you had a beautiful trot-canter transition, but it was one stride late and the judge gave you a score of 5 (where you had been repeatedly scoring 6's or 7's from other judges), don't panic. Also, don't starting "chasing" your horse into the transition. Instead, use this information constructively. It may just be a case whereby you should be asking for the transition one stride earlier or be clearer with your aids. Take the information and practice at home to find the solution.

Another interesting scoring nuance is revealed when you see the results of two different classes judged by the same judge. If the winning scores for both tests were in the high 50's, then it's quite likely that this judge is not overly generous, but that there were probably some nice rides. However, if the same judge awards the winning ride in one test a score in the high 60's or low 70's, and the winner of another test a 50%, then the rides in the second test were clearly not up to par.

If you discover a math error on your score sheet, you must bring it to the show manager's attention within one hour of the official posting of the scores from the last class of that show day.

Lameness and Drugs/Medications

Lameness

The AHSA rules regarding soundness give the judge the ultimate right and responsibility to eliminate a horse that she deems unsound. For under saddle classes, the AHSA rules state, "the horse must be serviceably sound for competition purposes." [The exception to this rule is stallions and mares competing in breeding classes only.] This means that the horse must not show signs of lameness, broken wind, or complete loss of sight in either eye. In the case of loss of sight in one eye, it is at the judge's discretion whether to deem the horse serviceably sound.

If a judge feels that a particular horse is lame, she may stop the rider during his test and excuse him. The rider may not appeal the decision and is eliminated from that test. However, this does not mean that the horse cannot compete later in the day. The horse may have suffered a minor bruise from stepping on a stone. If he is sound later in the day, the rider may compete in other tests for which he is entered.

Drugs and Medications

The rules surrounding drugs and medications are both extensive and complex. For more detailed information, refer to the *AHSA Rule Book,* or visit their website at http://www.ahsa.org, and review the General Rules section.

The AHSA's rules on drugs and medications fall into two categories:

- No Foreign Substance Group.
- Therapeutic Substance Group.

Both groups are explained in detail in the *AHSA Rule Book.* Because failure to comply with these rules can have a catastrophic effect on your horse's awards placings, you should consult the *AHSA Rule Book* for the most accurate and up-to-date information. The following are a few brief highlights:

Testing

At recognized competitions, a licensed veterinarian who is appointed by the Administrator of the Drugs and Medications Program may test any horse/ pony entered in the competition. This examination can include physical, urine, blood, and/or any other test deemed appropriate by the vet to determine whether a horse is on any type of medication.

Refusing to let your horse/pony be examined or non-cooperation with the veterinarian constitutes a violation and possible penalties to the responsible person. Competitors are responsible for cooperating with the veterinarian by making their horse/pony available to the vet for testing, by assisting the vet and his agent(s) in procuring samples, and by avoiding causing unnecessary delays to the vet.

Results

If the analysis of the samples taken from the horse (whether they are blood, urine, or other) indicate the presence of a forbidden substance, the competitor risks suspension from the AHSA, forfeiture of any prizes won (including prize money), points earned, and the horse/pony being barred from competition for a period of time.

Competitors should demonstrate extreme caution when using medicinal preparations, tonics, pastes, and products of any kind with which the ingredients and quantitative analysis are not specifically known. Many of these products contain one or more forbidden substances.

If you have questions regarding the interpretation of the drug rules as set forth in the *AHSA Rule Book*, contact the AHSA Drugs and Medications Program, 3780 Ridge Mill Drive, Hilliard, Ohio 43026-9231. (800)MED-AHSA, (614)771-7707, FAX (614) 771-7706

Care and Feeding of
the Dressage Competitor:
Your Horse and You

Both you and your horse are apt to be more physically and mentally taxed at a competition than you are when riding at home. For this reason, be sure to take proper care of your horse's needs as well as your own when at a competition.

Water for Your Horse

Water is the most vital "nutrient" for you and your horse; particularly during times of stress. Some horses are very sensitive to the odor and taste of unfamiliar water and may not be willing to drink water with which they are not familiar. If your horse is finicky, or if you have never taken him away from home and don't know how he'll react to a different water source, take water from home with you. Water can be stored in plastic gasoline cans (clearly marked "Water Only"), in plastic trash can liners that are inserted in water buckets and tied shut, or in plastic saddle racks that double as water containers. Check tack catalogs or with companies that manufacture

To reduce the risk of running out of the drinking water you brought from home, use show ground water to bath your horse, clean tack, wash your hands, etc.

farm supplies for the saddle rack/water containers. Plastic bags and even the water carrier may carry some residual smells and tastes that your horse won't like. Rinse the plastic containers repeatedly with water from the same source that you use to fill your horse's water buckets.

Another solution to the problem of unfamiliar smelling and tasting water is to add flavoring — apple cider, peppermint, apple juice, or Gatorade — to name a few. Try various flavorings to determine your horse's preferences. Certain flavorings may be just as unappealing to him as a different water source, so it's important to do your experimenting at home.

Horses customarily drink best from their own water buckets, and they seem to prefer light-colored buckets to dark. Take two buckets per horse with you to the show. If your horse doesn't go for flavored water, fill one bucket with water from home when you arrive at the show. Fill the other bucket halfway with show grounds water and halfway with water from home. This will help accustom your horse to unfamiliar water; this is especially important for shows that span several days in which it would be impractical to transport enough water to last the duration.

Another method for keeping your horse properly hydrated is to soak his feed. Soaked beet pulp is a good supplement to a horse's normal diet, and you can see how he likes it several days before the show. Try feeding him some very wet, sloppy beet pulp before the show; if he likes it, you can supplement his feed this way during the show. This will ensure that he is well hydrated for the trailer ride and at least the first several hours you are on the grounds. Grazing is also good for horses that are reluctant to drink. Fresh grass is loaded with electrolytes and water; the electrolytes will make him thirsty, and the water will help keep him hydrated. Most horses can't resist a bucket of cool, fresh water after an hour or so of grazing.

Place pieces of apple in your horse's water bucket so that he has to "bob" for them. This will frequently get a horse that was otherwise reluctant to drink unfamiliar water drinking. Another trick is to stand 5 or 6 carrots upright in the water bucket. Don't be afraid to experiment!

Checking Your Horse's Hydration — A Must

To check your horse's hydration, pinch a fold of skin on his neck above his shoulder. If the skin snaps promptly back in place, his hydration is excellent, and there's no need to worry. If the skin stays "tented" for a second or two, he is mildly dehydrated. If it "tents" for more than two or three seconds, he is becoming dehydrated. It's time to get some water into him, and call it quits for the day. Don't forget to try the skin pinching hydration test at home when you know your horse is well hydrated. Some horse's skin is looser than others, and older horses tend to have longer "tenting" than younger, fitter horses simply because their skin is not as elastic. You should be familiar with the characteristics of your horse's skin.

In addition to making sure that your horse is properly hydrated, it's also important that he be able to relieve himself. Many horses will not urinate in the trailer because they hate to splash themselves. Either put plenty of shavings on the trailer floor, or take your horse for a walk in tall grass where he'll find it more inviting to relieve himself.

Feed

Be sure to pack a sufficient supply of hay, and keep your horse's feeding schedule as close to normal as possible. Provide him with something to munch on while he's waiting in the trailer or standing in a stall between tests. If your horse is normally fed lunch, bring that along, too. You may have to alter his feeding schedule to accommodate your travel plans and your ride times. Since ride times are given at least several days in advance, it is not difficult to plan an adjusted feed schedule.

Upon arriving at the show, you may want to feed your horse some hay off the ground or let him graze. This aids in clearing his nasal passages and sinuses after a long trailer ride since many trailers don't give horses the option of being able to lower their heads.

Storing Your Horse's Food and Water

You will want to keep your horse's grain in a bucket that has a secure lid so that if it tips over while traveling, you don't lose any. Hay can be kept in a hay net, hay bag, or baled until you're ready to use it. Water can be stored as described earlier. On hot days, leave the wash bucket in the sun so that the water gets warm; however, keep the drinking water bucket under the truck or trailer to keep it cool. If you are showing out of your trailer and the weather is hot, try to find a shady spot in which to park.

Proper Hydration is a Must for You Too

You need proper food and hydration as much as your horse and neglecting your own needs will work against you when it comes time to ride. Many

A caveat regarding supplements — Carefully check the ingredients contained in any supplements that you feed your horse to be sure that none of them contain ingredients that are considered "forbidden substances" by the AHSA. Some forbidden substances are permitted as long as they are at a low enough level in the horse's system. It is the competitor's responsibility to get this information well in advance of a competition to avoid the possibility of being eliminated in the event your horse is drug tested.

people tend to take far better care of their horse's nutrition, hydration, and general wellbeing than their own, but just like your horse, your muscles will not work properly without sufficient hydration. Nor will your brain!

If you are fortunate enough to have a helper along with you, ask him to have a bottle of water ready for you so that you can have a last minute drink before heading down the centerline. A small bucket of water for your horse is advisable, too, or you can purchase a plastic bottle with lid and straw so that your helper can squirt some water into your horse's mouth to refresh him.

For several days prior to the show, drink more water than you might normally. Eight to ten 10-ounce glasses of water per day are not excessive. Don't wait until you are feeling thirsty to drink as this means that you are already somewhat dehydrated. Water is the best source of hydration since it contains no sugar that could upset your stomach.

Avoid all drinks containing alcohol or caffeine for at least 2 to 3 days prior to the show. Both act as diuretics and will rob you of much needed hydration. If you are not urinating frequently or your urine isn't clear, this is an indication that you are not drinking enough. Water, fruit juice, herbal ice teas, and watered-down Gatorade are your best bets. Gatorade contains sugar that could upset your stomach; so, it's best to dilute it with plain water.

Your Feeding and Comfort

It's not uncommon for first-time competitors to be quite conscientious about their horse's needs to the detriment of their own. There are little things that can make a big difference to your comfort and energy level. For instance, take along folding chairs, a tarp or other awning so that you can get out of the sun, and wear a sun visor or baseball hat when you can't be under cover. Keep your ice chest filled with ice and more cold drinks than you think you need. Have a pair of shorts and a T-shirt to change into in hot weather. In cold weather, have a change of clothes on hand that includes blue jeans (or other long pants), gloves, sweaters, warm socks, warm jacket, and so on. Your comfort is as important as your horse's. Not only will you be able to perform better if you attend to your own needs, but you will feel better and not tire as quickly.

Foods that are easy to transport and not apt to spoil are the best choices for horse shows. Simple, high-energy foods — granola bars, nuts, crackers, and fruit — are good choices. Avoid high sugar foods — candy bars, cookies, cakes — which tend to cause a "sugar crash" a short while after they're eaten.

Pay Attention to Your Own Needs

Hot weather can be just as debilitating and dangerous to you as to your horse. You should be aware of the signs of heat exhaustion and heat stroke so that you can take necessary action promptly. Although heat exhaustion is not life threatening on its own, it can cause you to faint, which is a safety factor when riding, not to mention being very uncomfortable. Signs of heat exhaustion are:

- Clammy, pale, damp skin.
- Feeling faint.
- Nausea, vomiting, diarrhea.

Heat stroke is a life threatening condition and must be treated as such. Symptoms of heat stroke are:

- Increase in body temperature because the victim's body ceases its efforts to cool itself.
- Sweating ceases.
- Skin is hot, DRY, and flushed.
- Victim is often delirious, often confused, and has little idea that he is in a life-threatening state.

The victim must be cooled as quickly as possible, and emergency medical attention sought. To reduce your risk of suffering from heat related illnesses, you can do the following:

- Get plenty of sleep or rest (more than you'd ordinarily need) before the competition.
- Spend time becoming acclimated to the hot environment (at least two weeks).
- Avoid alcohol, caffeine.
- Take frequent breaks.
- Drink plenty of water.
- Eat small meals frequently.

Between classes on a hot day, you should:

- Remove your jacket and helmet after dismounting.
- Find a cool, shady place to rest, or better yet, catch a catnap.
- Drink plenty of cool (not cold) beverages.
- Eat small snacks throughout the day.
- Take advantage of air-conditioned hotels, cars/trucks, and horse show offices whenever you can.

Your Comfort Checklist

Clothing

- ☑ Rainwear including rubber boots
- ☑ Shorts and tee shirts for hot weather
- ☑ Sweaters, blue jeans, warm socks, gloves, jacket for cold weather
- ☑ Extra shirts and pants in case something gets soaked
- ☑ Sun hat
- ☑ Sunglasses, sunblock

Food

- ☑ Cooler filled with ice
- ☑ Plenty of cold drinks
- ☑ Food of your choice
- ☑ Light snack foods
- ☑ Fruit
- ☑ Carrots for you and your horse
- ☑ Napkins, plates, plasticware, cups

Furniture

- ☑ Folding chairs for you, your helper, and others
- ☑ Tarp or awning for shade
- ☑ Box or small table to set food and drinks on

After the Show

Proper care of your horse after the show is crucial. Horses find competing just as stressful (maybe *more* stressful) than do their riders. They have been subjected to a new environment, strange sights, possibly more work than usual, and trailering to and from the show grounds.

What you do at the end of the day and the day after the show will go far toward maintaining your horse's well-being. There are some tasks you can perform before leaving the show grounds that will make him more comfortable. You can unbraid his mane if it was braided. Weather permitting, he should have been properly sponged off after each ride and a cooler put on if needed.

While waiting for your test results, get your truck packed, wrap your horse's legs, and apply the head bumper and tail bandage so that you can be on your way as soon as you have returned your number and picked up your score sheet. If you had a stall, be sure to clean it and retrieve anything that belongs to you, such as buckets, haynets, screw eyes and hooks, and the like.

Packing To Leave Checklist

- ☑ Unbraid mane
- ☑ Wrap legs
- ☑ Put on head bumper and tail bandage
- ☑ Pack up all equipment
- ☑ Get buckets and hay net out of stall if you had a stall
- ☑ Clean stall
- ☑ Return your number to the show secretary
- ☑ Pick up your score sheet(s)
- ☑ Have the show secretary sign your rider report form if you are working on a USDF Rider Awards or a Performance Certificate
- ☑ Check trailer hitch and lights
- ☑ Check that all trailer doors and tailgate are securely fastened
- ☑ Offer your horse another drink of water before heading out
- ☑ Check truck and trailer tires
- ☑ Make sure you didn't leave anyone behind

At Home At Last

Upon arriving home, put your horse in his stall before you do anything else so that he can relieve himself and have a drink of water. Then, remove his shipping clothes. A bran mash for dinner is a good idea as it will aid his digestion and help prevent colicking after a stressful day or weekend of competing.

The day after the show should be his day off, but be sure to check him over carefully and hand walk him for 15 to 20 minutes to loosen him up. Don't leave him standing idly in his stall all day. If he is accustomed to being turned out, keep him on his normal turnout schedule. Keep a close eye on him to be sure that he is eating and drinking normally.

This is also a good time to unpack and clean your equipment if you were too tired to do it the night before. File away your tests so that you can check them against AHSA and USDF records before season's end.

Sit down, breathe, and pat yourself on the back. You made it.

One of the kindest and best things you can do for your dressage partner is to turn him out on a daily basis. The Trakehner stallion Zauberklang clearly enjoys his liberty. Photo: Patricia L. Goodman

Much joy can be derived from raising your own performance horse. This well-bred and well-conformed filly went on to become a Grand Prix jumper under the show name "Crown Jewel!"

Celestia
Trakehner filly by Donauschimmer out of Celana
Photo: Patricia L. Goodman

USDF Awards Programs

There are a number of awards programs offered by the USDF to recognize the achievements of horses and riders at all levels. In addition, numerous breed organizations offer awards programs through the USDF. See *Appendix D* for a complete list of these organizations.

The USDF rider awards program acknowledges the achievements of riders all the way from Training level to FEI. To participate in the *Rider* awards programs, a rider must be a USDF member at the time the scores are earned. However, the horse does not have to be registered with the USDF.

Scores that count toward rider awards do not have to be earned in a single year; they can be earned over a period years. When the rider has attained the scores necessary for a particular award, he can send them to the USDF all at once.

For USDF awards programs that recognize a horse's achievements at the various levels (and awards offered by breed organizations), the horse must be registered with the USDF, and the owner, rider, and trainer must all be members of the USDF at the time the scores are earned.

The *USDF Horse of the Year* and *All Breeds* awards are yearly awards. Show management sends competition results to the USDF, and the USDF determincs year-end winners based on who has met all requirements and who has the highest median score at each level.

Each awards program is described in detail in the following pages. Pay special attention to the eligibility requirements for any awards that you are interested in pursuing.

For more information, contact USDF at P.O. Box 6669, Lincoln, NE 68506-0669. Telephone 402-434-8550, Fax 402-434-8570. You can also visit their web site at www.usdf.org.

An Important Message to Anyone Planning on Participating in USDF's Awards Programs

USDF awards and breed organization award rules and requirements can and do change frequently. Information presented here is from the USDF's 2000 Awards brochure Rev. 12/99. It is the competitor's responsiblity to read the most current awards program requirements carefully and abide by the mcmbership and competition requirements as set forth by the USDF and the participating breed organizations. You may contact them by phone, or by visiting their web site [www.usdf.org] for the most current information on awards programs.

Neither the USDF, Equissentials Press, nor the author may be held responsible in the event that a competitor, trainer, owner, rider, instructor or any other party associated with a competing horse neglects to check and abide by the most current rules and requirements surrounding the USDF's awards programs.

Rider Awards

USDF offers an awards program that acknowledges the accomplishments of riders at different levels. Scores that count toward these awards are cumulative and may be earned over a period of years; however, the award is presented in the year during which the final score is attained.

There are five USDF Rider Award programs. They are:

Qualified Rider   This award recognizes a rider's achievements at Training level.

Bronze Medal   This award recognizes a rider's achievements at First, Second, and Third levels.

Silver Medal   This award recognizes a rider's achievements at Fourth and Prix St Georges levels.

Gold Medal   This award recognizes a rider's achievements at Intermediaire and Grand Prix.

Master's Challenge   This award may be achieved at each level, Training through Fourth and FEI. Competitors must be age 60 or older as of December of the previous year.

Horses do not have to be registered with the USDF for their riders to participate in USDF's rider awards programs.

Eligibility

Eligibility requirements are the same for all of the above-mentioned awards with the exception of the Master's Challenge, which has an age requirement.

- The rider must be a USDF Group or Participating member at the time the scores are earned.
- The horse(s) do *not* have to be registered with USDF.
- The owner and trainer do *not* have to be USDF members.
- Membership begins when all application forms and fees are received by the USDF office.
- Scores may be earned on one or more horses.

Recorded Scores

- It is the rider's responsibility to submit scores to the USDF on official Rider Award Report forms. These forms are available directly from the USDF at no charge.
- The show secretary must sign the Rider Award Report form.
- If a rider is unable to obtain the show secretary's signature, he may send a photocopy of his test sheet to the USDF. The name and date of the show, the rider's name, and the judge's signature must be clearly visible. Do not send the original score sheet.
- Any score earned at a USDF/AHSA recognized competition in a regular AHSA or FEI test may be used with the exception of scores from freestyle and hors d'concours classes.
- If two or more judges score one ride, the average of their scores counts as one score.

Award Year

- Scores for all rider awards programs are cumulative and do not have to be earned in one year.
- Riders should submit their scores after all required scores have been earned. Do not submit your scores one at a time.
- All rides must be completed and reported to USDF by September 30 to be awarded in that year.

Qualified Rider Award Requirements

- Four scores of 60% or higher at Training level are required.
- Scores must be attained from at least two different competitions.
- Scores must be from four different judges.
- Scores must be for four different rides.
- A patch and certificate are awarded when the final score is reported.

Bronze Medal Award Requirements

- Six scores of 60% or higher are required.
- Two of the scores must be at First level from two different judges, for two different rides.
- Two of the scores must be at Second level from two different judges, for two different rides.
- Two of the scores must be at Third level from two different judges, for two different rides.
- The bronze medal and a certificate are presented at the Annual Convention.

Silver Medal Award Requirements

- Four scores of 60% or higher are required.
- Two of the scores must be at Fourth level from two different judges, for two different rides.
- Two of the scores must be at Prix St Georges from two different judges, for two different rides.
- The silver medal and a certificate are presented at the Annual Convention.

Silver Medal Score Equivalents for Jrs/YRs

- FEI Junior Preliminary Test = Third level, Test 2.
- FEI Junior Team and Individual tests, and Consolation tests = Fourth level.
- FEI Young Rider Individual Test = Prix St Georges.

Gold Medal Award

- Four scores of 60% or higher are required.
- Two scores must be at Intermediaire I and/or Intermediaire II from two different judges, for two different rides.

- Two of the scores must be at Grand Prix from two different judges, for two different rides.
- The gold medal and a certificate are presented at the Annual Convention.

Master's Challenge Award

- This award may be achieved at each level — Training through Fourth and FEI.
- The competitor must be age 60 or older as of December 1 of the previous year.
- The competitor must submit his birth date to the USDF before the end of the award year.
- Submit only scores that have been earned after January 1, 1990.

— Training, First, and Second Level Requirements —

- Four scores of 60% or higher are required.
- The scores must be from four different judges.
- The scores must be from four different rides.

— Third, Fourth, and FEI Level Requirements —

- Three scores of 55% or higher are required.
- The scores must be from three different judges.
- The scores must be from three different rides.
- FEI levels are combined. Scores may be earned from one level or any combination thereof.
- A certificate is presented at the Annual Convention.

Junior/Young Rider
Awards Program

USDF offers an awards program that acknowledges the accomplishments of junior/young riders. The following are the rules pertaining to USDF's Junior/Young Rider Awards program.

Eligibility

- The rider must be a USDF Participating member at the time the scores are earned.
- A junior/young rider must meet the AHSA dressage definition of junior/young rider as follows: a competitor is considered a junior/young rider until the end of the calendar year in which he or she reaches age 21.
- The junior/young rider must submit his/her birth date to the USDF before September 30th, which is the end of the award year.
- The owner of the horse (if someone other than the junior/young rider) must be a USDF Participating or Business member when scores are earned.

156

- The horse must be registered with the USDF at the time scores are earned.
- The horse and rider are considered a team for each level.
- Memberships and horse registrations begin when all application forms and fees are received by the USDF office.

Scores

- Scores are recorded directly from official competition results submitted by competition management.
- Check your scores occasionally throughout the year to make sure they have been recorded correctly. USDF will provide you with Score check forms at your request.
- Scores must be from FEI, AHSA, or USDF tests or score sheets that are current at the time of the competition and earned at USDF/AHSA recognized competitions.
- Hors d'concours scores do not count.
- If two or more judges are scoring one ride, the average of their scores will count as one score.
- Each ride will be recorded only once.
- All eligible scores are recorded. Freestyle scores are not recorded.
- The median score is the middle score. At Training, First, Second, Third, and Fourth levels, the top 80% of the scores are used to calculate the median score. The median score is the middle score.
- At Prix St Georges, Intermediaire I, Intermediaire II, and Grand Prix levels, if only four or five scores are recorded, all are used to calculate the median score. If six or more scores are recorded, the top 80% are used.

Score equivalents

- FEI Junior Preliminary Tests = Third level, Test 2.
- FEI Junior Team and Individual tests and Consolation tests = Fourth level, Test 1
- FEI Young Rider Team Test = Fourth level, Test 3
- FEI Young Rider Individual Test = Prix St Georges.

Competitions

Competitions that have previous performance requirements for entry eligibility are restricted competitions. Scores from these shows will not be applied toward USDF awards with the following exceptions:

- Scores from FEI classes at the following USDF/AHSA recognized competitions will be recorded: USET Selection Trials, CDIs, CDI-Ws, CDAs, Olympic Sports Festival, and Grand Prix National Championship.
- Scores from all ABIG/USDF Regional Championship classes.

Young rider Eliza Sydnor demonstrates an energetic trot on Maggie Georgiadis' Quarter Horse gelding, Double K. Double K is wearing polo wraps on his front legs, which are a good idea for schooling at home or warming up at shows. Wraps or boots can be used on all four legs if desired. Don't forget, though, neither boots nor wraps are permitted in competition. Photo: Cindy Sydnor

Requirements for Training through Fourth Levels

At Training through Fourth levels, the horse/rider team must earn a minimum of eight scores. For scores to count, you must adhere to the following rules:

- Scores must be earned from four different judges.
- Scores must be earned from four different shows.
- Scores must be from no more than two recognized competitions at the same location on consecutive days.
- Two of the scores must be from the highest test at that level (for ex-

ample, if you are competing at First level, two of the scores must be for First level Test 4). These scores must be 55% or higher.

- A rider must achieve a median score of 58% or higher to qualify.

Requirements for Prix St Georges, Intermediaire I, Intermediaire II, and Grand Prix Levels

At the FEI levels, the horse/rider team must earn a minimum of four scores. For scores to count, you must adhere to the following rules:

- Scores must be earned from four different judges.
- Scores must be earned from four different shows.
- Scores must be from no more than two recognized competitions at the same location on consecutive days.
- A rider must achieve a median score of 55% or higher to qualify.

Award Year and Presentation

- The award year begins on October 1st and ends on the following September 30th.
- No changes to award standings may be made after November 1st.
- Awards are presented at the Annual Convention.
- There are six awards at each level for Training through Prix St Georges.
- There are three awards at each level for Intermediaire I, Intermediaire II, and Grand Prix.
- Winners at each level qualify to win one-year's use of a Sundowner trailer and receive a cash award from the USDF/The Dressage Foundation.

Summary

To participate in USDF's Junior/Young Rider Awards program, be sure that you have the following in order:

- You are a Participating member of USDF at the time scores are earned.
- The owner of the horse you are riding (if other than you) is a USDF Participating or Business Member at the time scores are earned.
- The horse you are competing is registered with the USDF.
- Training through Fourth level riders must compete in at least four different shows, under four different judges.

- You must compete in the highest test of your level at least twice, and both scores must be 55% or higher.
- Submit your birth date to the USDF before the end of the award year (before September 30th).
- Save your test sheets and check your scores occasionally throughout the year to make sure that they have been recorded correctly. USDF will provide you with Score Check Forms at your request.

The Median Score Simplified

The middle score when you rank a group of scores from highest to lowest is called the median score. For example, say that a junior/young rider competing at First level earns the requisite 8 scores from 4 different judges at four different competitions. The scores have been ranked from highest to lowest as shown below:

1.	Test 1	68%
2.	Test 2	66%
3.	Test 1	65%
4.	Test 1	64%
5.	Test 3	63%
6.	Test 4	63%
7.	Test 2	61%
8.	Test 3	59%
9.	Test 4	58%
10.	Test 2	58%

Actual competition scores are carried out to three decimal places, but for the sake of simplicity, only whole numbers were used for this example.

As you can see, this rider has met the eligibility requirements for First level by earning a minimum of 8 scores and by scoring 55% or higher in both of her First level Test 4 rides (63% and 58% respectively). Since she has a total of 10 scores, and only the top 80% are used to calculate the median, scores 9 and 10 are dropped. This leaves an even number of scores from which to calculate the median. Scores 4 and 5 (the two middle scores) are added together and divided by two, resulting in a median score of 62.5% for this rider.

Adult Amateur Awards Program

USDF offers an awards program that acknowledges the accomplishments of Adult Amateur riders. An adult amateur rider is a competitor who is 22 years or older at the beginning of the calendar year and who meets the AHSA's definition of Amateur. Adult Amateurs must hold a current AHSA Adult Amateur card.

Refer to the *AHSA Rule Book* (Article 808. Amateur Status) for a detailed explanation of activities from which Adult Amateurs are restricted from engaging. Briefly, an Adult Amateur is someone who, after having reached his/her 21st birthday, does not accept payment for:

- Riding.
- Showing horses in hand, under saddle, or in harness.
- Training or schooling.
- Conducting clinics or seminars.
- Working as a secretary, bookkeeper, etc. for an equine organization.
- Allowing his/her name, photograph or any other type of personal association relating to his/her horse activities to be used commercially.
- Other (see the AHSA Rule Book for a more complete breakdown).

Activities that will not jeopardize an Adult Amateur's status include:

- Writing of books or articles pertaining to horses.
- Accepting payment for officiating as a judge, steward, technical delegate, course designer, or working as a veterinarian, groom, farrier, tack shop operator, or breeder, or bona fide remuneration for boarding services.
- Accepting payment for expenses without profit.
- Accepting a token of appreciation — other than money — for riding, driving or showing in halter or in hand. (Note: Horse board, prize money, partial support, or objects worth more than $300 are considered remuneration, not small tokens of appreciation. Also, accepting any amount of money, whether more or less than $300, is considered remuneration.)
- Having the occupation of veterinarian, groom, farrier; or owning a tack shop or breeding or boarding stable in itself, does not affect the amateur status of a person who is otherwise qualified.

Adult Amateur Certification

You do not have to join the AHSA to get an Adult Amateur card. However, if you do not join, there is a $30 fee (1999) for this card.

In order to compete as an Adult Amateur, a rider must have an Adult Amateur card issued by the AHSA. Riders may join the AHSA and complete the Adult Amateur form at no extra cost, or they may forego joining the AHSA and pay the $30 fee to obtain an Adult Amateur certificate.

Adult Amateurs must have their cards available to present at any AHSA/USDF recognized competition. If a rider forgets his card, he may sign an affidavit, which is sent to the AHSA for verification. Adult Amateur certification may be revoked at any time by the AHSA. Riders who violate any Adult Amateur rule will lose their certification and any awards they may have won while certified an Adult Amateur.

The following are the rules pertaining to USDF's Adult Amateur Awards program:

Eligibility

- The rider must be a USDF Participating member at the time the scores are earned.
- The rider must have a current AHSA Adult Amateur card and submit a

copy of it to the USDF before the end of the competition year (September 30th).

- The owner of the horse (if someone other than the adult amateur) must be a USDF Participating or Business member when scores are earned.
- Horses must be registered with the USDF at the time scores are earned.
- The horse and rider are considered a team for each level.
- Memberships and horse registrations begin when all application forms and fees are received by the USDF office.

Scores

- Scores are received directly from official competition results submitted by competition management.
- The median score is the score exactly between the highest and lowest within a specified range of scores.
- All eligible scores earned at USDF/AHSA recognized competitions within the award year are recorded. Freestyle scores are not recorded.
- Scores must be from FEI, AHSA, or USDF tests or score sheets that are current at the time of the competition and earned at USDF/AHSA recognized competitions.
- Scores must be from open, adult, adult amateur, or ABIG/USDF qualifying classes.
- Scores that are not eligible for inclusion in the Adult Amateur Awards program include tests that are ridden hors d'concours and competitions that have previous performance requirements for entry eligibility. These are restricted competitions and will not be applied toward USDF awards.

Exceptions to this are:

- Scores from FEI classes at the following USDF/AHSA recognized competitions: USET Selection Trials, CDIs, CDI-Ws, CDAs, Olympic Sports Festival, and Grand Prix National Championship.
- Scores from all ABIG/USDF Regional Championship classes.
- The Median score determines the year end total score.
- At Training, First, Second, Third, and Fourth levels, the top 80% of the scores are used to calculate the median.
- At Prix St Georges, Intermediaire I, Intermediaire II, and Grand Prix

levels, if only four or five scores are recorded, they are all used to calculate the median. If six or more scores are recorded, the top 80% are used.

- All scores are recorded directly from official competition results and are submitted by competition management.
- If two or more judges are scoring one ride, the average of their scores will count as one score.
- Each ride will be recorded only once.

Requirements for Training through Fourth Levels

At Training through Fourth levels, the horse/rider team must earn a minimum of eight scores. For scores to count, you must adhere to the following rules:

- Scores must be earned from four different judges.
- Scores must be earned from four different shows.
- Scores must be from no more than two recognized competitions at the same location on consecutive days.
- Two of the scores must be from the highest test at that level (for example, if you are competing at First level, two of the scores must be for First level test 4). These scores must be 55% or higher.
- A rider must achieve a median score of 58% or higher to qualify.

Requirements for Prix St Georges, Intermediaire I, Intermediaire II, and Grand Prix Levels

At the FEI levels, the horse/rider team must earn a minimum of four scores. For scores to count, you must adhere to the following rules:

- Scores must be earned from four different judges.
- Scores must be earned from four different shows.
- Scores must be from no more than two recognized competitions at the same location on consecutive days.
- A rider must achieve a median score of 55% or higher to qualify.

Award Year and Presentation

- The award year begins on October 1st and ends on the following September 30th.
- No changes to award standings may be made after November 1st.
- Awards are presented at the Annual Convention.
- There are six awards at each level for Training through Prix St Georges.
- There are three awards at each level for Intermediaire I, Intermediaire II, and Grand Prix.
- Winners at each level qualify to win one-year's use of a Sundowner trailer.

Summary

To participate in USDF's Adult Amateur Awards program, be sure that you have the following in order:

- You are a participating member of USDF at the time scores are earned.
- The owner of the horse you are riding (if other than you) is a USDF Participating or Business Member at the time scores are earned.
- The horse you are competing is registered with USDF.
- For Training through Fourth levels, you compete in at least four different shows, under four different judges.
- You must compete in the highest test of your level at least twice. For Training through Fourth levels, both scores must be 58% or higher.
- You must submit a copy of your Adult Amateur card to USDF before the end of the competition year (September 30th).
- Save your test sheets and check your scores occasionally throughout the year to make sure that they have been recorded correctly. USDF will provide you with Score Check Forms at your request.
- Be sure that the horse's owner (if someone other than you) signs your entry form.
- Be sure that you sign your entry form in the rider's signature block and the trainer's signature block unless you are going to have your trainer sign. If your trainer signs, he must be on the show grounds at the time you are competing.

Median Simplified

The median score is the middle score when you rank a group of scores from highest to lowest.

See the section entitled *Junior/Young Rider Awards Programs* for a detailed explanation of calculating median scores.

Vintage Cup Awards Program

USDF offers an awards program that acknowledges the accomplishments of riders who are 50 years old or older as of December 1st of the previous year.

The following are the rules pertaining to USDF's Vintage Cup Awards program:

Eligibility

- The rider must be a USDF Participating member at the time the scores are earned.
- The Vintage rider must submit his birth date to the USDF before the end of the award year (September 30th).
- The owner of the horse (if someone other than the Vintage rider) must be a USDF Participating or Business member when scores are earned.
- Horses must be registered with the USDF at the time scores are earned.
- The horse and rider are considered a team for each level.
- Memberships and horse registrations begin when all application forms and fees are received by the USDF office.

Scores

- All eligible scores earned at USDF/AHSA recognized competitions within the award year are recorded. Freestyle scores are not recorded.
- Scores must be from FEI, AHSA, or USDF tests or score sheets that are current at the time of the competition and earned at USDF/AHSA recognized competitions.
- Scores must be from open, adult, adult amateur (if eligible to ride as an Adult Amateur), or ABIG/USDF qualifying classes.
- Scores that are not eligible for inclusion in the Vintage Cup Awards program include tests that are ridden hors d'concours and competitions that have previous performance requirements for entry eligibility. These are restricted competitions and will not be applied toward USDF awards. *Exceptions to this are:*
  - Scores from FEI classes at the following USDF/AHSA recognized competitions: USET Selection Trials, CDIs, CDI-Ws, CDAs, Olympic Sports Festival, and Grand Prix National Championship.
  - Scores from all ABIG/USDF Regional Championship classes.
- The Median score determines the year end total score.
- At Training, First, Second, Third, and Fourth levels, the top 80% of the scores are used to calculate the median.
- At Prix St Georges, Intermediaire I, Intermediaire II, and Grand Prix levels, if only four or five scores are recorded, they are all used to calculate the median. If six or more scores are recorded, the top 80% are used.
- All scores are recorded directly from official competition results and are submitted by competition management.
- If two or more judges are scoring one ride, the average of their scores will count as one score.
- Each ride will be recorded only once.

Requirements for Training through Fourth Levels

At Training through Fourth levels, the horse/rider team must earn a minimum of eight scores. For scores to count, you must adhere to the following rules:

- Scores must be earned from four different judges.
- Scores must be earned from four different shows.
- Scores must be from no more than two recognized competitions at the same location on consecutive days.
- Two of the scores must be from the highest test at that level (for example, if you are competing at First level, two of the scores must be for First level test 4). These scores must be 55% or higher.
- A rider must achieve a median score of 58% or higher to qualify.

Requirements for Prix St Georges, Intermediaire I, Intermediaire II, and Grand Prix Levels

At the FEI levels, the horse/rider team must earn a minimum of four scores. For scores to count, you must adhere to the following rules:

- Scores must be earned from four different judges.
- Scores must be earned from four different shows.
- Scores must be from no more than two recognized competitions at the same location on consecutive days.
- A rider must achieve a median score of 55% or higher to qualify.

Award Year and Presentation

- The award year begins on October 1st and ends on the following September 30th.
- No changes to award standings may be made after November 1st.
- Awards are presented at the Annual Convention.
- There are three awards at each level for Training through Grand Prix.
- Winners at each level qualify to win one-year's use of a Sundowner trailer.

Summary

To participate in USDF's Vintage Cup Awards program, be sure that you have the following in order:

- You are a participating member of USDF at the time scores are earned.
- The owner of the horse you are riding (if other than you) is a USDF Participating or Business Member at the time scores are earned.

- Your horse is registered with the USDF.
- For Training through Fourth levels, you compete in at least four different shows, under four different judges.
- You must compete in the highest test of your level at least twice. For Training through Fourth levels, both scores from the highest test must be 58% or higher. For the FEI levels, the scores must be 55% or higher.
- Submit your birth date to USDF before the end of the competition year (September 30th).
- Save your test sheets and check your scores occasionally throughout the year to make sure they have been recorded correctly. USDF will provide you with Score Check Forms at your request.
- Be sure that the horse's owner (if someone other than you) signs your entry form.
- Be sure that you sign you entry form in the Rider's Signature block and the trainer's signature block unless you are going to have your trainer sign. If your trainer signs, she must be on the show grounds at the time you are competing.

Median Simplified

The median score is the middle score when you rank a group of scores from highest to lowest.

See the section entitled *Junior/Young Rider Awards Programs* for a detailed explanation of calculating median scores.

Dressage Horse of the Year Award

USDF offers an awards program that acknowledges the accomplishments of horses of any breed for each of the levels from Training through Grand Prix.

Eligibility

- The horse must be registered with USDF when the scores are earned.
- The owner must be a USDF Participating or Business member when the scores are earned.
- The rider must be a USDF Participating member when the scores are earned.
- Memberships and horse registrations begin when all application forms and fees are received by USDF office.

Scores

- Scores are recorded directly from official competition results submitted by competition management.
- The median score is the score exactly between the highest and lowest scores within a specified range of scores.
- Check your scores occasionally throughout the year to make sure they

have been recorded correctly. USDF will provide you with Score Check Forms at your request.

- Scores must be from FEI, AHSA, or USDF tests or score sheets that are current at the time of the competition and earned at USDF/AHSA recognized competitions.
- Hors d'concours scores do not count.
- If two or more judges are scoring one ride, the average of their scores will count as one score.
- Each ride will be recorded only once.
- All eligible scores are recorded. Freestyle scores are not recorded.
- At Training, First, Second, Third, and Fourth levels, the top 80% of the scores are used to calculate the median score. The median score is the middle score.
- At Prix St Georges, Intermediaire I, Intermediaire II, and Grand Prix levels, if only four or five scores are recorded, all are used to calculate the median score. If six or more scores are recorded, the top 80% are used.

Score Equivalents

- FEI Junior Preliminary Tests = Third level, Test 2.
- FEI Junior Team and Individual tests, and Consolation tests = Fourth level, Test 1
- FEI Young Rider Team Test = Fourth level, Test 3
- FEI Young Rider Individual Test = Prix St Georges

Classes

- Scores must be from open, adult, junior/young rider, adult amateur, or ABIG/USDF qualifying classes.

Competitions

Competitions that have previous performance requirements for entry eligibility are restricted competitions. Scores from these shows will not be applied toward USDF awards with the following exceptions:

1) Scores from FEI classes at the following USDF/AHSA recognized competitions will be recorded: USET Selection Trials, CDIs, CDI-Ws, CDAs, Olympic Sports Festival, and Grand Prix National Championship.

2) Scores from all ABIG/USDF Regional Championship classes.

Requirements for Training through Fourth Levels

- A minimum of eight scores are required.
- Scores must be from four different judges.
- Scores must be from four different competitions.
- Scores must be from no more than two recognized competitions at the same location on consecutive days.
- Two of the scores must be from the highest test of the level and be 55% or higher.
- The horse must have a median score of 58% or higher to qualify.

Requirements for Prix St Georges, Intermediaire I, Intermediaire II, and Grand Prix

- A minimum of four scores are required.
- Scores must be from four different judges.
- Scores must be from four different competitions.
- Scores must be from no more than two recognized competitions at the same location on consecutive days.
- The horse must have a median score of 55% or higher to qualify.

Award Year and Presentation

- The award year commences on October 1 and ends the following September 30.
- No changes to award standings may be made after November 1.
- Awards are presented at the Annual Convention.
- Twenty awards are presented at each level for Training through Intermediaire I.
- Fifteen awards are presented at Intermediaire II and Grand Prix.
- Winners at each level receive a cooler sponsored by State Line Tack and qualify to win one year's use of a Sundowner trailer.
- The Grand Prix Horse of the Year receives the Colonel Thackeray Award as well as a silver trophy and wool cooler sponsored by Impac.

All-Breeds Awards

USDF offers an awards program that acknowledges the accomplishments of horses registered with participating breed registries for each level from Training through Grand Prix. See *Appendix D* for a list of breed organizations that participate in the USDF All-Breeds Awards program.

Eligibility

- The horse must be registered with USDF when the scores are earned.
- The owner must be a USDF Participating or Business member when the scores are earned and is responsible for checking with his breed organization to be sure that he meets that organization's membership requirements.
- The rider must be a USDF Participating member when the scores are earned.
- Memberships and horse registrations begin when all application forms and fees are received by USDF office.
- A photocopy of the breed registration must be submitted to USDF before the end of the award year (September 30th).

Check directly with your breed organization to be sure that you and your horse meet all of their competition and membership requirements as they relate to the USDF awards program.

- The horse must be registered with and meet all requirements of the sponsoring breed organization.

Scores

- Scores are recorded directly from official competition results submitted by competition management.
- The median score is used to place horses. The median is the score exactly between the highest and lowest scores within a specified range of scores.
- Check your scores occasionally throughout the year to make sure they have been recorded correctly. USDF will provide you with Score Check Forms at your request.
- Scores must be from FEI, AHSA, or USDF tests or score sheets that are current at the time of the competition and earned at USDF/AHSA recognized competitions.
- Hors d'concours scores do not count.
- If two or more judges are scoring one ride, the average of their scores will count as one score.
- Each ride will be recorded only once.
- All eligible scores are recorded. Freestyle scores are only recorded for Freestyle awards. The median score is the middle score.
- At Training, First, Second, Third, and Fourth levels, the top 80% of the scores are used to calculate the median score. The median score is the middle score.
- At Prix St Georges, Intermediaire I, Intermediaire II, and Grand Prix levels, if only four or five scores are recorded, all are used to calculate the median score. If six or more scores are recorded, the top 80% are used.
- Scores must be from open, adult, junior/young rider, adult amateur, or ABIG/USDF qualifying classes, OR from the same classes restricted to horses of the particular breed.
- If scores are earned in both types of classes, the combination of the scores is used to calculate the median score.
- Classes restricted to horses of a particular breed must be judged by an AHSA licensed dressage judge.

Competitions

Competitions that have previous performance requirements for entry eligibility are restricted competitions. Scores from these shows will not be applied toward USDF awards with the following exceptions:

1) Scores from FEI classes at the following USDF/AHSA recognized competitions will be recorded: USET Selection Trials, CDIs, CDI-Ws, CDAs, Olympic Sports Festival, and Grand Prix National Championship.
2) Scores from all ABIG/USDF Regional Championship classes.

Requirements for Training through Fourth Levels

- A minimum of eight scores are required.
- The scores must be from four different judges.
- The scores must be from four different competitions.
- The scores must be from no more than two recognized competitions at the same location on consecutive days.
- Two of the scores must be from the highest test of the level and be 55% or higher. For example, if you are competing at Third level, two of your scores must be from Third level Test 3 and be at least 55%.
- The horse must have a median score of 58% or higher to qualify.

Requirements for Prix St Georges, Intermediaire I, Intermediaire II, and Grand Prix

- A minimum of four scores are required.
- The scores must be from four different judges.
- The scores must be from four different competitions.
- The scores must be from no more than two recognized competitions at the same location on consecutive days.
- The horse must have a median score of 55% or higher to qualify.

Award Year and Presentation

- October 1 through September 30th.
- No changes to award standings may be made after November 1st.
- Awards are presented at the Annual Convention.

- Breed organizations may award up to five certificates per level and division and give other prizes at their discretion. If division awards (such as freestyle, adult amateur, etc.) are offered, rules pertaining to that division must be fulfilled.

Cosequin®/USDF
Musical Freestyle Awards

USDF offers an awards program that acknowledges the accomplishments of horses competing in musical freestyle competitions.

Eligibility

- The horse must be registered with USDF when the scores are earned.
- The owner must be a USDF Participating or Business member when the scores are earned.
- The rider must be a USDF Participating member when the scores are earned.
- Memberships and horse registrations begin when all application forms and fees are received by the USDF office.

Scores

- Scores are recorded directly from official competition results submitted by competition management.
- The median score is the score exactly between the highest and lowest

scores within a specified range of scores.

- Check your scores occasionally throughout the year to make sure they have been recorded correctly. USDF will provide you with Score Check Forms at your request.
- Scores must be from FEI, AHSA, or USDF tests or score sheets that are current at the time of the competition and earned at USDF/AHSA recognized competitions.
- Hors d'concours scores do not count.
- If two or more judges are scoring one ride, the average of their scores will count as one score.
- Each ride will be recorded only once.
- Non-freestyle scores are not used to calculate the freestyle median score, but rather as a qualifying tool to demonstrate the horse's ability to perform movements required at that level.
- If only three or four scores are recorded, they are all used to calculate the median score. If five or more scores are recorded, the top 80% are used.

Requirements for First through Fourth Level Freestyles

- A minimum of three freestyle scores are required.
- Scores must be from three different judges.
- Scores must be from three different competitions.
- Scores must be from no more than two recognized competitions at the same location on consecutive days.
- Two non-freestyle scores of 55% or higher at the highest test of level OR at any test at next-highest level are required.
- The horse must have a median score of 58% or higher to qualify.

Requirements for Intermediaire I and Grand Prix Freestyles

- A minimum of three freestyle scores are required.
- Scores must be from three different judges.
- Scores must be from three different competitions.
- Scores must be from no more than two recognized competitions at the same location on consecutive days.
- Two non-freestyle scores of 55% or higher at standard test of FEI level

OR next-highest level are required.

- The horse must have a median score of 55% or higher to qualify.

Award Year and Presentation

- October 1 through September 30th.
- No changes to award standings may be made after November 1st.
- Awards are presented at the Annual Convention.
- Three awards at each level for First, Second, Third, and Fourth levels.
- Six awards at each level for Intermediaire I and Grand Prix.
- Winners at each level receive cash prizes sponsored by Cosequin®.

Performance Certificates

USDF offers an awards program that acknowledges the accomplishments of horses competing at each level from Training through Grand Prix.

Eligibility

- The horse must be registered with USDF when the scores are earned.
- The owner must be a USDF Participating or Business member when the scores are earned.
- There are no membership requirements for the rider.
- Memberships and horse registrations begin when all application forms and fees are received by USDF office.

Scores

- The owner is responsible for submitting scores to USDF using a Performance Certificate Application that is available from USDF.
- A copy of each test and/or a USDF score printout must be submitted with each application.
- Scores are verified by USDF from official competition results.

- Any score earned at a USDF/AHSA recognized competition in a regular AHSA or FEI test may be used excluding freestyle or hors d'concours.
- If two or more judges score one ride, the average of their scores counts as one score.

Requirements for All Levels

- Certificates may be earned at every level.
- Ten scores of 60% or higher are required.
- Scores must be from four different judges, from four different competitions.
- Four of the scores must be from the highest test of the level at which the horse is competing.
- There is a $25 fee payable to USDF for each level certified.

Award Year and Presentation

- The owner must submit all ten scores together using a Performance Certificate Application.
- Scores are cumulative and do not have to be earned in one year.
- A completed application and fee must be submitted by September 30th for inclusion in current awards year.
- Certificates are issued as received and verified by USDF.

USDF Regional Championships

Each year USDF organizes regional dressage championships in all nine USDF regions (see *Appendix B* for a listing of regions). These championships are recognized by the AHSA. Although Alaska is in Region 6 and Hawaii in Region 7, they may hold their own state championships.

Each region must offer USDF Regional Championship classes at each level (except Introductory) up to and including Intermediaire I in three divisions: Open, Adult Amateur, and Junior/Young Rider. At Intermediaire II and Grand Prix, only Open champions may be named; there are not separate divisions for Adult Amateur and Junior/Young Rider.

Freestyles at First through Fourth levels, Intermediaire I, and Grand Prix must also be offered in the Open division. If freestyle classes are combined, championships must be awarded at each level competed. Dates and locations of the Regional Championships are available from USDF after January 1st of the New Year.

Qualifying Rules

To compete in a Regional Dressage Championship, riders must adhere to the USDF's qualifying system. Rules for qualifying, as of 1999, are as follows:

1) The nationally standardized qualifying system of minimum percentages is used. See the table on the next page.

2) Horse/rider combinations must earn a total of two qualifying scores in official ABIG/USDF Qualifying Classes, at two different AHSA/USDF recognized shows, from two different judges.

3) To qualify riders must enter an official ABIG/USDF Qualifying Class at AHSA/USDF recognized competitions which offer the ABIG/USDF Qualifying Classes. The ABIG/USDF Qualifying Class will be the highest test of the level (e.g. First level Test 4, Third level Test 3, and so on). The Competition Secretary is responsible for sending the Qualifying ride fee of $10 to USDF.

4) Multiple day shows may offer one qualifying class per level/division per day.

5) Any and all horse/rider combinations who achieve the minimum qualifying score in an ABIG/USDF Qualifying Class will receive one qualifying score toward their two score requirement to be eligible to enter a Regional Championship. Riders do not need to win the class to be qualified.

6) To qualify at Freestyle, riders must earn a total of two freestyle qualifying scores at the level at which they wish to compete. These scores must be earned in official ABIG/USDF Qualifying Classes at two different AHSA/USDF recognized competitions, from two different judges.

7) FEI classes at CDA, CDI, or CDI-W competitions will be considered as ABIG/USDF Qualifying Classes. If riders in those classes wish the score to be considered as a qualifying score, they must either pay a $10 ABIG/USDF Qualifying Class fee per class to the competition secretary for a Regional Championship, or they must send a $10 ABIG/USDF Qualifying Class fee per class to USDF along with a copy of the test.

8) All horse/rider combinations may receive qualifying scores in any region. The rider must enter the ABIG/USDF Regional Championships in his/her own region unless declaration of change of Region has been made to the USDF office by July 1st of the Championship year.

Competitors who have met all of the qualifying, membership, and entry requirements for a particular regional championship cannot be denied entry into the regional championship classes for which they have qualified.

9) There is no limit on the number of horses a rider may qualify.

10) Qualification is based on horse/rider combination.

11) All persons who have qualified and entered by the closing date must be allowed to compete in the Championship Classes.

12) Rules for Qualifying: Whips may be carried when qualifying, except in FEI recognized competitions, USET Championships Qualifying and Selection Trials, and Observation Classes. Whips must be within regulation length as defined in the AHSA *Rule Book,* that is, a whip may be no more than 4' in length including the lash.

13) Tests may be read, except in FEI level and Freestyle classes.

14) The qualifying season will vary for each region. The season during which qualifying scores may be earned for a particular Regional Championship is from the closing date of that region's previous Championship year, to the closing date of that region's current Championship year. The closing date must be four weeks prior to the Championship event.

15) Competition secretaries will send the results of the ABIG/USDF Qualifying Classes to USDF, along with the $10 per ride fee. USDF will deposit the funds received from the ABIG/USDF Qualifying Classes, less an administration fee, into a restricted fund earmarked for The National Dressage Championships.

16) USDF will maintain a database of qualified horse/rider combinations. A list of qualified horse/rider combinations will be sent to each region's designated Championship contact person.

Competitors do not need to win their qualifying class in order to qualify. Instead, they must meet the qualifying score requirements as shown in the table below.

Minimum Qualifying Scores

	Open	AA	Jr/YR
Training Level	65%	60%	60%
First Level	65%	60%	60%
Second Level	63%	59%	59%
Third Level	60%	57%	57%
Fourth Level	60%	57%	57%
Prix St Georges	60%	57%	57%
Intermediaire I	60%	57%	57%
Intermediaire II	58%	N/A	N/A
Grand Prix	58%	N/A	N/A

Freestyle	Open	AA	Jr/YR
First Level	65%	N/A	N/A
Second Level	65%	N/A	N/A
Third Level	65%	N/A	N/A
Fourth Level	63%	N/A	N/A
Intermediaire I	63%	N/A	N/A
Grand Prix	63%	N/A	N/A

Championship Eligibility

1) The rider must be a US citizen.
2) The horse/rider combinations that have won a USDF Regional Championship since 1994 may no longer compete in USDF Regional Championship competition in that division, at that level or a lower level with the exception of Grand Prix. Championship records prior to 1994 will not be considered.
3) A horse may not be entered in more than one USDF Regional Championship at a particular level in the same calendar year.
4) Riders are not required to be a resident of a particular region to compete in that region's championship. USDF will assume qualified horses will compete in the region in which the rider resides. Riders who wish to declare a region other than their region of residence should contact the USDF office by July 1st of the Championship year.

Membership/Registration Requirements for Qualifying and Championships

Rider:

- Must be a USDF Participating member at the time qualifying scores are earned.
- Must be an AHSA member (Junior, Senior, or Life) at the time the qualifying scores are earned.

Horse:

- Must be USDF registered at the time qualifying scores are earned.
- Horse must be AHSA recorded at the time qualifying scores are earned.
- The horse does not have to be registered with any breed organization.

Owner:

- Must be a USDF member (Participating or Business) at the time qualifying scores are earned.
- Must be an AHSA member (Junior, Senior, or Life) at the time qualifying scores are earned.

Championship Rules

1) Riders must declare on the championship entry form for each level, if the horse/rider combination is competing in the Open, Adult Amateur, or Junior/Young Rider division, and must meet minimum percentage requirements for the championship division entered.

2) Any horse entered in a USDF Regional Championship competition, even if entered at two levels, must be ridden by the same rider throughout the competition. Therefore, a horse can only be ridden by one rider.

3) Cross-entering divisions within one level is not allowed. For example, a horse/rider combination could not enter First Level Adult Amateur and First Level Open. However, a horse/rider combination may enter First Level Open and Second Level Adult Amateur.

4) If a rider enters a championship as an Adult Amateur, she must be an adult by the current AHSA definition (see *Glossary*), and a current Amateur by the AHSA definition (see *Glossary*). The rider must submit a photocopy of her Adult Amateur card to USDF by July 1st of the championship year, and submit a photocopy of her Adult Amateur card with the championship entry.

5) Riders intending to enter a championship as a Junior/Young Rider must be a Junior/Young Rider by the current AHSA definition (see *Glossary*) and must submit their birth date to USDF by July 1st of the championship year.

6) Photocopies of USDF membership cards must accompany championship entry (USDF Participating Membership for rider, USDF Participating or Business Member for owner).

7) No whips will be carried in championship tests, except by competitors riding side saddle.

8) All championship tests must be ridden from memory.

9) At no time during a USDF Regional Championship competition may any horse entered in the competition be ridden by anyone other than the rider entered in the Championship competition on that horse (the one

Participating members are USDF members who join USDF directly instead of through their GMO's.

exception to this is grooms riding on a loose rein).

10) In the event of a tie for Champion or Reserve Champion, the Collective Marks will determine 1st, 2nd, and 3rd place. Otherwise, a tie will remain unbroken.

Membership/Registration Requirements at the Time of the Championship

The horse registration requirements are the same as required for qualifying. The only difference in the membership requirement is that at the time of the championship, the rider must be a USDF Participating Member. Members who join USDF through a local club (GMO) are Individual Members, and must join the USDF directly as Participating Members.

Prize Money

1) Should sponsorship money be available for use as prize money in 1999 and in subsequent years, it will be distributed evenly among the regions.

2) Each region shall divide its share of prize money equally among classes offered; this includes all classes in all three divisions (Open, Adult Amateur, and Junior/Young Rider). 60% of the amount per class shall go to the Champion, and the remaining 40% shall go to the Reserve Champion.

3) Beginning 12/1/98, the Qualifying fee will be $10 per class entered. $5 from each qualifying fee will be deposited in a prize money fund. Beginning in the year 2000, all money accumulated during the AHSA competition year (December 1-November 30), shall be divided equally among all USDF regions and shall be distributed as per number 2 above.

An Important Message to Anyone Planning on Competing in USDF Regional Championship Competitions

Rules and requirements surrounding USDF Championship Competitions can and do change frequently. It is the competitor's responsiblity to read the most current USDF Regional Championship competition requirements carefully and abide by the membership and competition requirements as set forth by the USDF. You may contact them by phone, or by visiting their web site [www.usdf.org] for the most current information on their Regional Championships.

Neither the USDF, Equissentials Press, nor the author may be held responsible in the event that a competitor, trainer, owner, rider, instructor, or any other party associated with a competing horse neglects to check and abide by the most current rules and requirements surrounding the USDF's Regional Championship competitions.

Appendix A
Judge's Designations

The AHSA, USDF, and FEI offer programs for aspiring judges as well as certification that acknowledges a person's successful completion of the programs.

A particular letter (as described below) is assigned to a judge to indicate the training they have received and the levels that they can judge.

L   "L" stands for *learner*. Learner judges are just beginning their judging careers and must pass a test (with a score of 85% or better) given by the USDF in order to pursue the AHSA judge's ratings as described below (r, R, and S). L judges can judge schooling and USDF league competitions.

r   An "r" judge is a *recorded* AHSA judge who is licensed by the AHSA to judge through Second level.

R   An "R" judge is a *Registered* AHSA judge who is licensed by the AHSA to judge through Fourth level.

S   An "S" judge is a *senior* judge and can judge any AHSA/USDF tests through the FEI levels. S judges can judge all levels but only at U.S. competitions.

C   A "C" judge is a judge who is an FEI *candidate*. This is the first step to becoming an international judge at all levels. C judges can judge any level as well as qualifying classes for international Games as a panel member.

I   An "I" judge is an FEI *International* judge. I judges can judge any level as well as the selection trials for international competitions. They will preside at C on the panel.

O   An "O" judge is an FEI *Official* and can judge tests of any level at any competition. O judges are the only judges who can judge Olympic competitions, World Cups, and World Equestrian Games and are invited to do so with no financial remuneration.

Appendix B
USDF Regions

Region One
- Delaware
- District of Columbia
- Maryland
- New Jersey
- North Carolina
- Pennsylvania
- Virginia

Region Two
- Illinois
- Indiana
- Kentucky
- Michigan
- Ohio
- West Virginia
- Wisconsin

Region Three
- Alabama
- Florida
- Georgia
- South Carolina
- Tennessee

Region Four
- Iowa
- Kansas
- Minnesota
- Missouri
- Nebraska
- North Dakota
- South Dakota

Region 5
- Arizona
- Colorado
- Montana (zipcodes excluding 59400-59499, 59600-59999)
- New Mexico
- Texas (zipcodes including 79800-79999)
- Utah
- Wyoming

Region 6
- Alaska
- Idaho
- Montana (zipcodes including 59400-59499, 59600-59999)
- Oregon
- Washington

Region 7
- California
- Nevada
- Hawaii

Region 8
- Connecticut
- Maine
- Massachusetts

New Hampshire
New York
Rhode Island
Vermont

Region 9
Arkansas
Louisiana
Mississippi
Oklahoma
Texas (zipcodes excluding 79800-79999)

Appendix C
Highlights of Show
Rules and Regulations

It probably won't surprise you to learn that there are a number of rules and regulations that must be followed at dressage shows, and failure to adhere to the rules can result in elimination. AHSA/USDF recognized competitions adhere to rules as defined by the AHSA. Most schooling shows choose to follow AHSA rules as well.

Earlier chapters of this book covered correct attire for horse and rider, a list of legal and illegal equipment, how to complete an entry form, hints on warming up, and more. The following are a few crucial tips that bear repeating, as well as a list of the grounds for elimination.

Competitors must adhere to all of the show's rules from the time they arrive on the showgrounds until their departure.

Tips

1) You have 60 seconds in which to enter the ring once the judge has rung the bell. Failure to enter the arena in this time period will result in elimination.

2) You cannot be required to ride before your scheduled ride time. If you are scheduled to ride at 10:20 a.m. and the show is running 10 minutes ahead of time, show management cannot make you ride early. However, if you are warmed up and ready to go, you have the option of riding at the earlier time.

3) In the event of something unusual occurring, such as a loose horse running past or through the arena in which you are competing, the judge may stop your test and let you restart it from the beginning or whatever point she deems appropriate.

4) Be sure your horse's number is on his bridle any time you are working him whether it be longeing, warming up, or competing.

5) Remember to remove your horse's boots or leg wraps before entering the arena.

6) If you are riding a test that does not permit a whip, be sure to drop it

before entering the arena. If a whip is permitted, be sure that it is no longer than 4' in length including the lash.

Grounds for Elimination

- Failure to enter the arena within 60 seconds of the bell being rung.
- Misrepresentation of an entry or an inappropriate entry. An example of misrepresentation of an entry would be a professional competing in an amateur class.
- Use of illegal equipment. Martingales, draw reins, and the like are considered illegal equipment. See the chapter entitled *Dressing Your Horse for a Show* for a detailed list of illegal equipment.
- Unauthorized assistance. The intervention by a third party to facilitate the riding of your test is considered unauthorized assistance.
- Four errors of the course. Each time a rider goes off course, she is penalized. The first error results in a deduction of 2 points, the second error is a deduction of 4 points, the third error is a deduction of 8 points, and the fourth error results in elimination. Be sure that you have memorized your test thoroughly or have a reliable reader. Three errors will lower your score by a full 14 points!
- Horse's tongue tied down. It is illegal to tie a horse's tongue down, and any competitor who does so will be eliminated.
- All four feet of the horse leave the arena. If the horse should step (or jump) out of the arena with all four feet, he will be eliminated.
- Cruelty. The AHSA has an in-depth description of what constitutes cruelty in their *General Rules* book. It includes withholding food or water from an animal, letting blood from a horse for other than diagnostic purposes, excessive use of the spurs or whip, etc. Refer to the AHSA's *General Rules* book for more specifics.
- Marked lameness. The judge or President of the Jury may eliminate a rider if they deem that his/her horse is lame. This decision may not be appealed.
- Resistance of longer than 20 seconds. If a horse should refuse to perform a movement for 20 seconds or longer, he will be eliminated.
- In an FEI Freestyle class, performing movements that are not allowed.
- Removing one's helmet at any other time except to salute the judge will lead to elimination.
- Freestyle competitors may perform movements included at or below

the level in which their freestyle is designed. However, if they perform a movement from a level above, they will be eliminated.

- Any situation where a direct rule violation can be cited. If a violation cannot be cited, a competitor will not be eliminated.
- Errors due to mistakes by a reader (caller) do not relieve the rider from error penalties if she goes off course.
- Carrying a whip that is more than 4' in length including the lash.
- Carrying whips in classes that don't permit whips.
- Illegal use of drugs.

Numerous other rules exist, and every competitor should avail themselves of the AHSA's various rule books.

You can find the entire AHSA rule book and changes to rules on their web site at www.ahsa.org.

Appendix D
Breed Organizations Participating
in USDF Awards Programs

American Bashkir Curly Registry
Sue Chilson
371 Clark Street
Ely, NV 89301

Tel. 702-289-4999
Fax 702-289-8579

American Connemara Pony Society
Marilyn DeWispelaere
32 30th Street #A
W. Palm Beach, FL 33407

Tel. 561-804-9284

American Donkey & Mule Association
Leah Patton
2901 N. Elm
Denton, TX 76201

Tel. 817-382-6845

American Hanoverian Society
Hugh Bellis-Jones
4059 Iron Works, Bldg. C
Lexington, KY 40511

Tel. 606-255-4141
Fax 606-255-8467
ahsoffice@aol.com

American Holsteiner Horse Association
Carol Biesenthal
5039 W. Stephenson Road
Freeport, IL 61032

Tel. 815-235-4031
Fax 502-868-0722
holsteiner@igc.apc.org

American Morgan Horse Association
Desiree DeVries
122 Bostwick Road
Shelburne, VT 05482

Tel. 802-985-4944
Fax 802-985-8897
info@morganhorse.com

This list of breed organizations that participate in the USDF's award program was current as of January, 2000. Contact the USDF or your breed organization to be sure that your breed organization is still offering awards through USDF and to check for any changes to rules or requirements.

American Mustang & Burro Assn. Inc.
George Berrier
1151 Pacific Avenue
Rio Oso, CA 95674

Tel. 530-633-9271
Fax 916-632-1855

American Paint Horse Association
Linda Knowles
P.O. Box 961023
P.O. Box 961023
Fort Worth, TX 76161

Tel. 817-439-3400
Fax 817-439-3484
www.apha.com

American Performance Horse Assn.
Eileen Updyke
1530 Colesville Road
Harpursville, NY 13787

Tel. 607-693-3133

American Quarter Horse Association
1600 Quarter Horse Drive
Amarillo, TX 79104

Tel. 806-376-4811
www.aqha.com

American Saddlebred Horse Association
Paula Birney Thoroman
1500 W. Edwards
Springfield, IL 62704

Tel. 217-693-1590
Fax 217-483-2235

American Trakehner Association
Helen K. Gibble
20520 Falcons Landing Circle Apt. #2408
Sterling, VA 20165

Tel. 703-404-4590
Fax 703-404-4591
hkgib@aol.com

American Warmblood Registry
Marion O'Connor
P.O. Box 46
Careywood, ID 83806

Tel. 208-683-3255
Fax 208-683-3255
soujakl@aol.com

American Warmblood Society
Jean Brooks
6801 W. Romely Avenue
Phoenix, AZ 85043-6906

Tel. 602-936-6621
Fax 602-936-4790

Appaloosa Horse Club
Joanne Marble
5070 Hwy. 8 West
Moscow, ID 83843

Tel. 208-882-5578
Fax 208-882-8150
journal@appaloosa.com

Appaloosa Sport Horse Association
Mary Lou Wiskowski
1360 Saxonburg Boulevard
Glenshaw, PA 15116

Tel. 412-767-4616

Arabian Sport Horse Association
Pamela Turner
Shibui Ni Farm
6145 Whaleyville Boulevard
Suffolk, VA 23438

Tel. 757-986-4486

Belgian Warmblood Breeding Assn.
Norma Inqui
900 N. Mildred Street
Ranson, WV 25438

Tel. 304-725-8840
Fax 304-725-1924

Cleveland Bay Horse Society of NA
Faye Mulvey
Porridge Hill
27 Hoxsie Road
West Kingston, RI 02892

Tel. 401-539-8272
Fax 401-539-8272
porridgehillcb@juno.com

Dutch Warmblood NA-WPN
Silvia Monas
P.O. Box O
Sutherlin, OR 97479

Tel. 541-459-3232
Fax 541-459-2967
nawpn@rosenet.net

Friesian Horse Association of NA   Tel. 970-484-2079
Carolyn Handeland   Fax 970-484-4321
2950 S. County Road 5
Fort Collins, CO 80525

Friesian Horse Society, Inc.   Tel. 281-375-8815
Evelyn Vollmer-Prohaska   Fax 281-934-3115
Rt. 1, Box 80V
Brookshire, TX 77423

Haflinger Breeders Organization, Inc.   Tel. 978-546-3748
Mrs. Mimi Smith   Fax 978-546-6329
85 South Street
Rockport, MA 01966

Hungarian Horse Association   Tel. 308-749-2411
Wanda Cooksley
HC 71, Box 108
Anselmo, NE 68813

International Andalusian & Lusitano   Tel. 805-589-3195
Horse Association   Fax 805-589-6933
13109 Hageman Road
Bakersfield, CA 93389

International Arabian Horse Association   Tel. 303-696-4500
Carol Alm   Fax 303-696-4599
10805 E. Bethany Drive   iaha@iaha.com
Aurora, CO 80014-2605

International Buckskin Horse Association   Tel. 219-552-1013
Dolores Kurzeja   Fax 219-552-1013
3517 West 231st Avenue
Lowell, IN 46377

International Sporthorse Registry
Carol Richardson
939 Merchandise Mart
Chicago, IL 60654

Tel. 312-527-6544
Fax 312-527-6573
isreg@aol.com

Lipizzan Association of NA
Melody Hull
110 E 700 N
Alexandria, IN 46001

Tel. 765-644-3904
Fax 765-641-1205
thull@iquest.net

National Show Horse Registry
Robert Peebles
11700 Commonwealth Drive
Suite 200
Louisville, KY 40299

Tel. 502-266-5100
Fax 502-266-5806

New Forest Pony Association & Registry
Lucille S. Guilbault
362 Wakefield Road
Pascoag, RI 02859

Tel. 401-568-8238
Fax 401-568-0311
nfpony@hotmail.com

North American Selle Francais Horse
Association, Inc.
Sheryl L. Van Gundy
P.O. Box 646
Winchester, VA 22604

Tel. 540-662-2870
Fax 540-662-3628
glenasfa@shentel.net

North American Shagya-Arabian Society
Gwyn Davis
9797 South Rangeline Road
Clinton, IN 47842

Tel. 765-665-3851

North American Trakehner Association
Kathy Gilbertson-Smock
P.O. Box 12172
Lexington, KY 40581

Tel. 502-867-0375
Fax 502-867-1820

Norwegian Fjord Horse Registry
Lindsay Sweeney
RR #1, Box 134
Tunbridge, VT 05077

Tel. 802-889-3735
nfhr@frontiernet.net

Oldenburg Registry North America
Carol Richardson
939 Merchandise Mart
Chicago, IL 60654

Tel. 312-527-6544
Fax 312-527-6573
isreg@aol.com

Palomino Horse Breeders of America, Inc.
Cindy Chilton
15253 E. Skelly Drive
Tulsa, OK 74116-2637

Tel. 918-438-1234
Fax 918-438-1232
yellahrses@aol.com

Performance Horse Registry
Laura Smith
821 Corporate Drive
Lexington, KY 40524-4710

Tel. 606-224-2880
Fax 606-224-2710

Pinto Horse Association of NA
Marlene Pankow
1900 Samuels Avenue
Fort Worth, TX 76102-1141

Tel. 817-336-7842
Fax 817-336-7416

Pony of the Americas Club, Inc.
Jean Donley
5240 Elmwood Avenue
Indianapolis, IN 46203

Tel. 317-788-0107
Fax 317-788-8974
Poac@iquest.net

Purebred Hanoverian Association
Barbara Dressler
RD 8, Cherry Hill Road
Princeton, NJ 08540

Tel. 609-466-1383
Fax 609-466-9543

Swedish Warmblood Association
Kristina Paulsen
711 Grasser Hill Road
Coupeville, WA 98239

Tel. 360-678-3503
Fax 360-678-3023

Thoroughbred Horses for Sport
Diana Clarke
10808 Georgetown Pike
Great Falls, VA 22066

Tel. 703-759-6273
Fax 703-759-4676

United States Lipizzan Registry
George Williams
Tempel Farms
17000 Wadsworth Road
Wadsworth, IL 60083

Tel. 847-244-5330
Fax 847-244-5069
uslroffice@aol.com

Welsh Pony & Cob Society of America, Inc.
Gayle Day
20281 FM 1385
Pilot Point, TX 76258

Tel. 817-686-5667
wpcsa@crosslink.net

Appendix E
Arena Figures

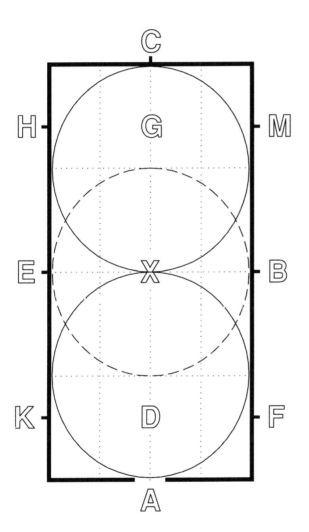

20 meter circles that commence at A, C or X are the full width of the arena and exactly half the length. The dotted line indicates a 20 meter circle commencing at either E or B.

The small arena is 20 meters wide by 40 meters long or approximately 66 feet by 132 feet.

20 meter circles in a small arena

A 20 meter circle starting at E or B. The dotted line between E and B indicates a half circle. If the test calls for a half circle from B to E, start the half circle at B, proceed to E as shown, and then proceed straight ahead as indicated by the dotted line.

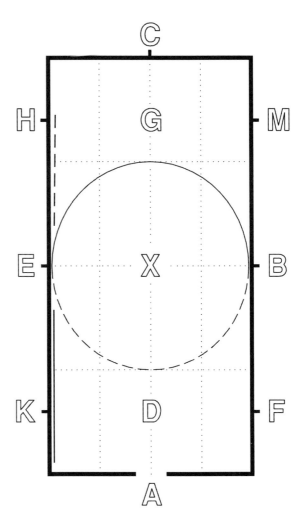

The 20 meter circle and half-circle between E and B in a small arena

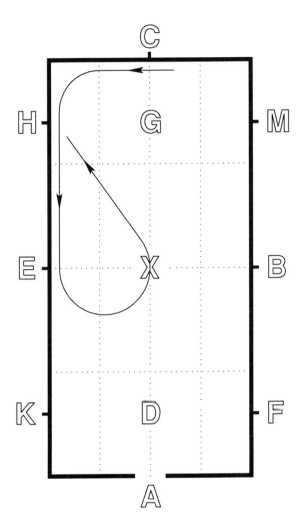

Half-circles to change the rein (direction) appear at First level. As you can see by this drawing, the turn commencing at E is 10 meters in width.

First level tests are typically held in the standard arena rather than the small arena as shown here.

A half-circle from E to H to change the rein

212

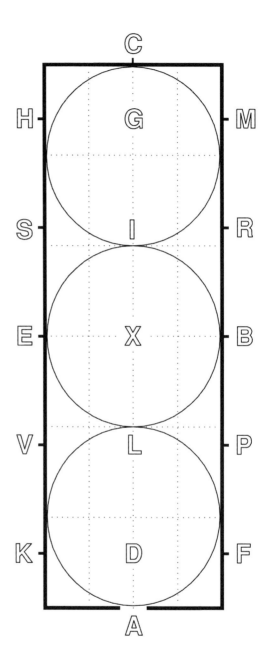

The placement of 20 meter circles when performed in a standard arena.

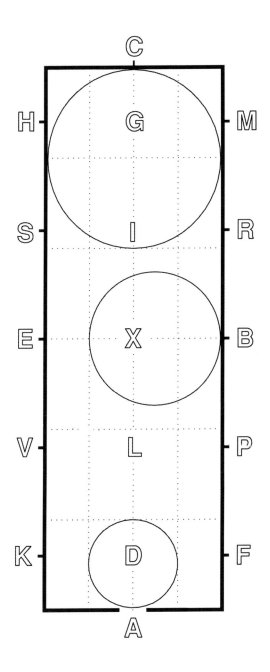

A 20 meter circle starting at C (as shown), is the width of the arena.

A 15 meter circle beginning at B would take you to the quarter line closest to E as shown here.

A 10 meter circle beginning at A (as shown) or at C, touches each of the quarter lines. A 10 meter circle starting at any of the outside markers (e.g. E, S, B, etc.) would touch the center line.

Various sized circles

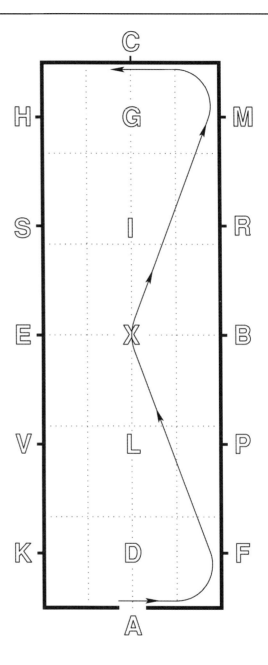

A loop from F to X to H. This can be performed in the walk, trot, or canter depending upon the level at which you are competing.

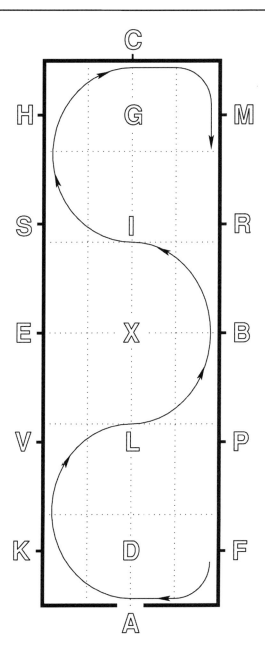

A three loop serpentine

A 15 meter circle at C.

A 10 meter circle beginning at B touches the center line and is completed when the horse reachs B.

8 meter circles at P and at A.

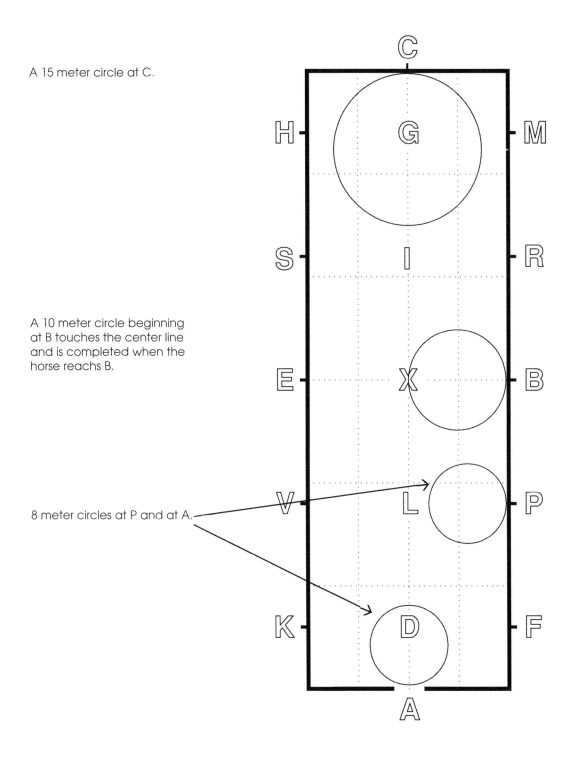

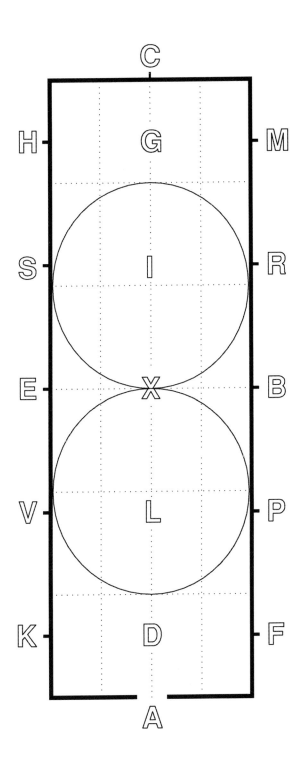

20 meter circles originating at X.

Appendix F
Important Contact Information

American Horse Council
1700 K Street, N.W.
Washington, DC 20006-3805

Tel. 202-296-4031

American Horse Shows Association
(AHSA)
220 East 42nd Street
New York, NY 10017-5876

Tel. 212-972-2472
Fax 212-983-7286
www.ahsa.org

Federation Equestre Internationale
(FEI)
Avenue Mon-Repos 24
P.O. Box 157CH-1000
Lausanne 1
SWITZERLAND

Tel. 011-41-21-312-5656
Fax 011-41-21-312-8677

United States Dressage Federation, Inc.
(USDF)
P.O. Box 6669
Lincoln, NE 68506-0669

Tel. 402-434-8550
Fax 402-434-8570
www.usdf.org

United States Equestrian Team
Gladstone, NJ 07934

Tel. 908-234-9417
Fax 508-698-6811

Glossary

ABIG   American Bankers Insurance Group. The spon-
                              soring organization for AIBG/USDF year end
                              championships.

Adult   For the current awards year, competitors are con-
                              sidered to be adults from the beginning of the
                              calendar year in which they reach age 22.

Adult amateur class   A class that is open to adults who meet the AHSA
                              dressage definition of adult or adult amateur.

Adult amateur   A rider who is 18 years of age or older as of De-
                              cember 1 of the current competition year, does
                              not receive remuneration for riding, driving,
                              showing in-hand, training, schooling, conduct-
                              ing clinics or seminars; and holds a current AHSA
                              Amateur card. A copy of a rider's AHSA Amateur
                              card must accompany his/her entry to be eligible
                              for awards in the Adult Amateur division. See the
                              AHSA book *General Rules* for more detailed in
                              formation.

Adult amateur card   A card verifying that a rider meets the qualifica-
                              tions for competing as an amateur. Riders must
                              fill out the appropriate AHSA form, include the
                              required payment, and apply directly to the AHSA
                              for an Adult Amateur card.

AHSA   American Horse Shows Association. AHSA writes
                              the rules for dressage competitions as well as the
                              Training through Fifth level tests that are used in
                              U.S. dressage competitions.

AHSA levels   The AHSA dressage levels are Training, First, Sec-
                              ond, Third, and Fourth.

Arena	The enclosed area in which dressage competitors ride. There are two sizes of arena: the small arena which is 20-meters by 40-meters, and the standard arena which is 20-meters by 60-meters. Arenas are enclosed with low wooden or chain fences.
Bell	A bell, whistle, or other sounding device is used for two reasons: to warn a rider that they have one minute in which to begin their test, and to stop a rider during a test.
Breed/discipline fee	This is a fee charged by the AHSA to competitors who are entering AHSA recognized competitions but are not AHSA members. This fee is determined by the AHSA annually. Junior non-members are exempt from paying this fee.
Caller	A person who reads the test to a rider. Also, known as a reader. Callers may not be used at any Final or Championship Event. Competitors are responsible for making arrangements for a person to call (read) the test.
CDA	Concours Dresseur Amitie — a "friendly" dressage competition. Not more than four foreign countries may compete in a CDA.
CDI	Concours Dresseur International — an international dressage competition.
CDI-O	Concours Dresseur International Officiel — Official International dressage competition.
CDI-W	Concours Dresseur International — an international dressage competition that is a sanctioned World Cup Qualifier event.
Certificate of Capability	A certificate that riders wishing to compete in the Olympic games must have. To obtain this certificate, riders must submit to the USET two scores of at least 60% earned in the Grand Prix from

any FEI Official International Dressage Judge (FEI "O" judge) who is not a U.S. citizen, at two different CDI***/CDI-W's within a certain time period.

CHIO — Concours Hippique International Officiel – Official International Equestrian Competition. This type of competition has more than one discipline with most member countries being permitted one "official" international competition in each discipline. (Aachen is one of the most well-known CHIO's in the world).

Closing date — The last date at which an entry form may be postmarked. Entries submitted after this date are considered post entries and may or may not be accepted at the discretion of the show management.

Coefficient — A multiplier that is assigned to a particular movement. For instance, if a rider scores a 7 for a movement that has a coefficient of 2, the score then becomes 14.

Coggins test — A test for the highly contagious disease, Equine Infectious Anemia (EIA). Competitions require that the competing horse has tested negative within the last 12 months (in some cases, within the last 6 months).

Collective marks — The marks at the bottom of the test sheet. There are four individual collective marks, and they include: gaits, impulsion, submission, and rider's seat and position. Collective marks in Training level through Grand Prix tests all carry a coefficient of 2.

Competition year — The USDF's competition year begins on October 1st and ends on the following September 30th.

Depressant — A substance that depresses the cardiovascular, respiratory, or central nervous systems of the horse. *See* "Forbidden substance."

Directives	These are the instructions on the test sheet that tell the judge and the rider what particular quality is being sought in each movement.
Dressage derby	A contest in which the riders should expect to change horses. It is conducted in two parts: 1) the rider rides a special test; 2) the four highest-scoring riders are then given the opportunity to warm-up for the same length of time on one another's horses and ride the test again. The winning rider is the rider with the highest total score (four rides).
Dressage equitation class	This class is open to all riders. Exhibitors will perform at the medium walk, working trot, and canter in both directions with other competitors, but may be required by the judge to perform individually. The rider's seat, position, and correct use of the aids required by the Training and First level dressage tests are judged. Riders are not asked to change horses. Riders may wear spurs and carry a whip but must use a plain snaffle. No more than 15 entries are permitted.
Entry form	The form a rider must complete and send to the show secretary on or before the closing date in order to enter a dressage competition. Each region's Omnibus contains two copies of the official entry form. It is the competitor's responsibility to make additional copies of the entry form.
FEI	Federation Equestre Internationale. This is the international governing body of equestrian events. The FEI is responsible for writing and administering rules for international competitions and for writing the international level dressage tests (i.e. Prix St Georges, Intermediaire I, Intermediaire II, Grand Prix, and Grand Prix Special).

FEI levels	The FEI levels are Prix St Georges, Intermediaire I, Intermediaire II, Grand Prix, and Grand Prix Special. The same tests are used worldwide.
Final Selection Trials	The final selection trials are the two competitions at Gladstone that determine which horse/rider combinations will make up the U.S. Olympic dressage team. Invitations to the final selection trial are determined by the average of all scores in the Grand Prix tests from qualifying competitions. The 12 horse/rider combinations with the highest average scores are invited to compete in the final selection trials.
Footing	The surface of any area where you work your horse (e.g. sand, rubber, grass, Fibar, etc.)
Forbidden substance	Any stimulant, depressant, tranquilizer, local anesthetic, psychotropic (mood and/or behavior altering) substance, or drug which might affect the performance of a horse and/or pony.
Freestyle	A test that is designed by the rider and ridden to music of the rider's choice. The rider determines what level the freestyle is and must incorporate all of the movements required at that level into his/her test.
Gatekeeper	The person who oversees the opening and closing of the competition arena gate. (Note: there is no rule that requires that the gate be closed.)
GMO	Group Member Organization of the USDF. Local- level dressage clubs that organize schooling shows and clinics. Contact the USDF to find the GMO nearest you.
Ground jury	The ground jury is the judge or judges officiating at a competition. They are trained to judge according to a standard as opposed to comparing one horse to another. Judges must be licensed to

officiate at AHSA or FEI competitions. See *Appendix A* for a detailed description of the various judge's ratings.

Health certificate

Some shows require that a veterinary health certificate be obtained within a certain number of days before the show. This certificate is presented to show management prior to unloading your horse from your trailer/van.

Hors de Concours

A rider may choose to ride a test hors d' concours. This means that she will pay all appropriate fees and follow all competition rules, but the score will not count towards a prize or year-end awards. Typically, riders ride hors d'concours when they want to get some mileage on a horse or try a new test. A rider must get permission from the show management to ride hors d' concours before the beginning of the class in which he plans to compete.

IOC

International Olympic Committee. The international governing organization for the Olympic games. Olympic games are held every four years — on the leap years for the summer games and the two years in between for the winter games.

Judge

See Ground jury.

Junior rider

A person may compete as a junior from the beginning of the calendar year in which she reaches the age of 14 until the end of the year in which she reaches the age of 18. Juniors are automatically considered amateurs.

Junior/Young rider class

A class that is open to juniors and young riders who meet the AHSA definition of Junior/Young Rider. For the current awards year, a competitor is a Junior/Young Rider until the end of the calendar year in which he/she reaches age 21.

Letters	The markers around the perimeter of the arena on which letters are painted.
Levels	The levels start with USDF Introductory level, which is the most basic level. AHSA Training through Fourth levels are next, and finally the FEI levels, which culminate at Grand Prix, the most advanced level of all.
Limit class	Limit classes are open to horses that have not won six first places at an AHSA recognized dressage competition.
Long list	This is a list drawn up by the USET Dressage Committee and approved by the USET Executive Committee of rider/horse combinations whose outstanding competitive records indicate that they are the strongest candidates for future teams and therefore eligible for USET training programs and other USET recognition.
Maiden class	Maiden classes are open to horses that have not won a first place at an AHSA recognized dressage competition.
Musical freestyle	Musical freestyles are rides that are designed by the competitor and ridden to music selected by the competitor. Freestyles are judged both on technical skill and artistic merit.
NF	National Federation. Each country has its own national federation; our national federation is the American Horse Shows Association (AHSA).
(N)OC	National Olympic Committee. Every country has its National Olympic Committee member of the IOC.
Non-member fee	This is a fee that a competitor must pay when entering an AHSA recognized competition if she is not an AHSA member. The fee amount is included on the official entry form that is provided

with the Omnibus.

Novice class	Novice classes are open to horses that have not won three first places at an AHSA recognized dressage competition.
Omnibus	A book that is printed annually and is available for each of the nine USDF regions. It includes prize lists for every USDF/AHSA recognized competition within the region. Along with information on each individual show are information on championships, year-end awards, copies of the tests, and two entry forms.
Open class	A class that is open to all. There are no restrictions based on the horse (age, breed, sex, size, previous performance, residence or membership of owner) or rider (age, experience, qualifications, sex, residence, or membership).
Opening date	This is the earliest date that an entry may be postmarked for a competition. If a competition lists its opening date as May 1st, the postmark on the entry form envelope must be May 1st or later.
Owner	The recorded owner of the horse must sign the "Owner" signature block on the entry form. For a horse to be eligible for AHSA Horse of the Year Awards, at least one owner (assuming the horse has more than one owner) must be an AHSA Individual Senior Active, Junior Active, or Life Member.
Participating member	A USDF member who joins the USDF directly rather than through a GMO. She pays dues annually (as opposed to a life member). A participating member is eligible to participate in any USDF awards programs including breed awards as long as she and her horse are properly recorded and registered with a breed organization.

Pas de Deux	A test in which two horse/rider combinations perform an original ride from memory simultaneously. At the final bell, riders must advance to G and salue together. The Pas de Deux is judged on similarity as a pair, ability to perform together, composition of the ride, and execution of the ride.
Post entry	Post entering is the act of entering a show after the posted closing date. This may only be done with permission of the show management, and there is usually an additional fee for post entries. Post entries may occasionally be made on the day of the competition if another competitor scratches (withdraws) from a class thereby leaving an opening.
Prize list	A detailed description of a particular competition. It includes a list of the classes offered and judges who will be officiating, as well as information on stabling, hotel accommodations, arena footing, warm-up areas, and costs.
Professional	Any person who receives remuneration for riding, driving, showing in-hand, training, schooling, conducting clinics, or seminars.
Quadrille	A test ridden by a group of riders – typically eight. They design their own test and must adhere to the rules set forth by the USDF.
Qualifying class	Classes offered at recognized US competitions that riders can enter in order to earn the necessary scores to qualify to compete a particular horse at a particular level in the year end championship show in their region. Not to be confused with qualifying competitions.
Qualifying competitions	*See* Selection trials.
Recognized show	A competition that is sanctioned by the AHSA and/ or the FEI. Recognized shows must hire licensed

judges who are listed in the AHSA's or FEI's list of judges licensed to judge dressage competitions. All AHSA rules must be adhered to. Scores from recognized shows are used by USDF to calculate their year-end awards.

Reader	*See* Caller.
Rhythm	Rhythm refers to the number of beats in each gait. The walk is a four-beat gait, the trot is a two-beat gait, and the canter is a three-beat gait.
Ring steward	Ring stewards have dual roles; they keep riders apprised of how many horses are ahead of them in their test, and they check saddlery and equipment at the Technical Delegate's request.
Runner	A horse show worker who transports test sheets or other important information between the judge and the show office.
Salute	At the beginning of the test and again at the end, the rider salutes the judge by bowing her head slightly and dropping one hand to her side. *See* the chapter entitled *Saluting* for more detail.
Schooling show	A schooling show is a small competition that is not recognized by the AHSA or USDF. Schooling shows are primarily for the purpose of introducing horses and/or riders to the competition scene. Some clubs offer a series of schooling shows with year-end awards. Schooling shows typically have lower entry fees because show management is not required to hire licensed judges.
Scorer	A person(s) who calculates and posts test scores. In the case of an incorrect score, you should contact the show manager or the secretary; not the scorer.
Scratch	Withdraw from a class. No refunds are available on entries that are scratched after the show's clos-

ing date. Entries scratched before the closing date and with a veterinarian's certificate are given a refund less an office fee, as specified on the prize list for that show.

Scribe
A person who sits next to the judge and records the judge's comments and scores on the test sheet.

Selection trials
USET designated competitions (also known as qualifying competitions) across the country in which riders can earn the needed scores to qualify for the final selection trials. Riders must compete in at least two qualifying competitions in order to be considered for the final selection trials.

Short List
A short list of up to five riders and up to eight horses selected to travel to and compete in Europe prior to the Olympic games. Selections are made based on the highest average percentage scores from the final selection trials held at Gladstone.

Show manager
The person(s) who oversees the organization, smooth running, and adherence to AHSA/FEI regulations of a dressage competition. They are responsible for hiring judges, renting stabling (if needed), hiring nightwatchmen, answering questions about entries and much more.

Show secretary
The schow secretary receives all entries and is responsible for checking that all signature blocks have been signed, all necessary health certificates and membership cards are included, and money for entry fees and stabling are enclosed. Once she has finished this task and the closing date goes by, she schedules the rides.

Stimulant
A substance that stimulates the cardiovascular, respiratory or central nervous systems. *See* "Forbidden substance."

Technical delegate	A technical delegate (TD) is an official AHSA representative who is an advisor to competitors as well as competition management and makes sure that AHSA rules are followed. If you have any questions regarding competition rules or would like permission to speak with the judge, this is the person you contact. TD's help to clarify rules, but they do not enforce them. An "R" technical delegate is a Registered technical delegate and may officiate alone at AHSA/USDF championships, and USET championships, qualifying and selection trials and observation classes at any dressage competition or in the dressage division or section at recognized or local member shows. "r" is a recorded technical delegate and may not officiate alone at the competitions at which an R technical delegate can officiate. But, an r technical delegate may act as the assistant to an R and can officiate at other competitions such as schooling shows.
Tempo	The speed at which the horse's feet touch the ground and can be measured in bpm (beats per minute) using a metronome.
Trainer	Any adult who is responsible for caring for, training, or who has custody of a show horse. This person must sign the entry form of any recognized competition in the space provided. Competitors who are juniors or young riders and don't have a trainer, must have their parent or guardian sign the space designated "Trainer." The owner and/or rider can sign the trainer's signature block.
Training scale	See the chapter entitled *The Purpose of the Movements* for an explanation of the training scale.
USDF	United States Dressage Federation. Thousands of individuals as well as local dressage clubs na-

tionwide comprise the USDF and benefit through this association in a number of ways. USDF is responsible for numerous awards programs as described in the Awards chapters. Visit their website at http://www.usdf.org for detailed information.

USET   United States Equestrian Team.

Vintage rider   Defined by the USDF as a rider who is age 50 or older as of December 1st of the previous year. A vintage rider must submit his/her birth date to the USDF before the end of the award year in order to participate in the Vintage Cup Awards. These awards are described in detail in the Awards chapter.

Whistle   A whistle (bell, or any other sounding device) may be used to alert the rider that he should begin his test, or that he has made an error during the test.

Young rider   Individuals are eligible as Young Riders from the beginning of the calendar year in which they reach the age of 16 until the end of the calendar year in which they reach the age of 21. Competitors shall compete as Adults from the beginning of the calendar year in which they reach the age of 22.

Index